PRAISE FOR *YOUR BRAIN ON FACTS*

T0006922

"A fun collection of facts that will leave you full of information you never knew you needed to know!"

—Sophie Stirling, author of *We Did That?*

"Like most seekers of knowledge, I am always searching out unusual and unique books on a wide range of topics. If you are the same, look no further than *Your Brain on Facts*. If you love the eponymous podcast, then you know that Moxie is a relentless and excellent purveyor of hidden history and long-lost facts. Read enough of this book and you'll be the most popular person at any cocktail party!"

—Alicia Alvrez, author of *The Big Book of Women's Trivia*

"I like to read this book for ten to fifteen minutes every night before bed or when I first wake up in the morning. It has bite-sized nuggets of information I have never seen anywhere else. I love how author Moxie LaBouche has uncovered so many random events in history and facts on everything obscure. She is an excellent researcher and this book delivers big on delight!"

—Becca Anderson, author of *Badass Affirmations*

"*Your Brain on Facts* cannot describe this book (and the podcast on which it's based) more accurately! Once you open the book, the facts hit you at full speed. Moxie doesn't hold back her trivia-filled brain. She is a natural sponge for knowledge, and I am so happy she gets to squeeze all that knowledge—well, maybe only a portion of how much she actually knows—into a full book! I'm looking forward to reading this over and over again and leaving it out for my kids because these are the types of books that will keep them curious for years to come. This is truly a book that belongs in any trivia lovers' house."

—Emily Proko, podcaster and author of *The Story Behind*

"If you are looking to entertain your brain with some unusual facts, you will love *Your Brain on Facts*. Moxie's humorous delivery of the facts keeps you turning the page. I love learning something new every time I read the book!"

—Joyce Glass, The Write Coach

"I've been a fan of Moxie's Twitter feed for a while now…but it's even nicer to have all of these delightful facts and stories packaged in book form! Thumb through the pages, pause anywhere, and I'm certain you'll find something that not only tickles your brain, but makes you smile too."

—Mangesh Hattikudur, cofounder of Mental Floss

"LaBouche's witty writing, along with the smorgasbord of facts, makes this book a must-read for family trips, classrooms, and should claim the coveted spot on the bathroom reading shelf. LaBouche bring fun back to learning. I highly recommend this book for every coffee table, waiting room, and break room. You will walk away laughing and learning."

—Cherrilynn Bisbano, author of *Shine, Don't Whine*

"Moxie LaBouche takes readers on an adventure through several well-researched categories of facts and trivia. There's plenty to learn here, perfect for beginners or the most devoted of trivia fans who enjoy their facts with a dash of humor. Enjoy choice information from the owner of *Your Brain on Facts* podcast, like Vsauce in novel form."

—Elise Hennessy, author of the Blood Legacy series

YOUR BRAIN ON FACTS

YOUR BRAIN ON FACTS

Things You Didn't Know,
Things You Thought You Knew,
and Things You Never Knew You
Never Knew

MOXIE LaBOUCHE

CORAL GABLES

Published by Mango Publishing Group, a division of Mango Media Inc.

Cover Design, Layout & Design: Morgane Leoni
Cover Illustration: © Meranna/shutterstock.com

For permission requests, please contact the publisher at:
Mango Publishing Group
2850 S Douglas Road, 2nd Floor
Coral Gables, FL 33134 USA
info@mango.bz

For special orders, quantity sales, course adoptions and corporate sales, please email the publisher at sales@mango.bz. For trade and wholesale sales, please contact Ingram Publisher Services at customer.service@ingramcontent.com or +1.800.509.4887.

Your Brain on Facts: Things You Didn't Know, Things You Thought You Knew, and Things You Never Knew You Never Knew

Library of Congress Cataloging-in-Publication number: 2020933907
ISBN: (print) 978-1-64250-253-4, (ebook) 978-1-64250-254-1
BISAC category code GAM012000, GAMES & ACTIVITIES / Trivia

Printed in the United States of America

To my mother,
for supporting all of my endeavors,
even the really stupid ones.

CONTENTS

FOREWORD

●

Humans are weird. I am raising two small humans, and they remind me of this fact on a daily basis. But aside from the obvious idiosyncrasies we all have, humans are also weird because we are the only species that questions the world around us.

Cats don't stop to wonder why they land on all fours. They just do it and move on.

But humans couldn't just accept that as fact. We questioned it for hundreds of years, probably to the detriment of many cats who were unwilling participants in these trials. It wasn't until we had new technology that we were finally able to watch a cat using what's now known as his Righting Reflex to maneuver his body so he can land on all four paws.

And we, weird humans that we are, probably celebrated this new knowledge while the first cat ever to be recorded on video went along his day probably thinking to himself, "Humans are weird!"

But that's what makes us human. Some doctors even think our ability to wonder "why?" about the world around us separates us from every other species.

And that's amazing! (And a boost to our egos, who are we kidding?)

Until you remember that ignorance exists. And that there are people in the world who are blissfully living in it.

Another funny thing about humans is even though questioning the world around us is something we naturally are inclined to do, it's often frowned upon and many of us are trained at a young age *not* to question what we're taught.

Luckily, Moxie LaBouche probably never listened to that and even if she heard it, she probably questioned it right away.

We also have a tendency to avoid our "weirdness," and follow the crowd, maybe mirroring the actions, language, or even thoughts of others around us. Anything so we can blend in until we can figure out how our own personal brand of "weirdness" fits into the world.

We also tend to surround ourselves with those who share many of our same thoughts, ideas, and values, which might give us the false impression that the rest of the world is just like us.

It might not even be on a large scale—it may just be that your favorite social media app adjusted its algorithm to your liking so much that you've inadvertently surrounded yourself with an echo chamber of those who post things similar to things you've already liked and posted yourself.

Anyone who has studied history can back me up on that. Some pretty terrible things have happened in the world when humans decided that "weird" was no longer good and it was decidedly better to be like those with the most power or money or who come from a particular region or speak a certain way.

Ignorance may be bliss, but it's not necessarily good.

Maybe no one will ever give the Nobel Peace Prize to someone for their contributions to bar trivia as we know it, but I do think that trivia can lead to great conversations.

Trivia can be a wake-up call from the past. In the not-so-distant past, for example, bacon was "doctor-approved" as a healthy breakfast. Cigarettes, which were seen as patriotic for men to smoke but unladylike for women to be seen with, got a marketing makeover when a far-fetched Freudian theory was used to spin them into a symbol of feminism. But going deeper into those stories—which Moxie does in this book—you may start questioning what products today have used similar advertising tactics. As soon as you begin to question that, you are no longer a victim of ignorance.

One of the most intelligent statements someone can make is admitting that they don't know what they don't know. Sometimes just admitting that can be intimidating, but it also means you're open to learning more. And, as many historians will tell you, we can't hope for a better future unless we learn from the past.

So tickle your brain, but don't forget to share your knowledge with others! Trivia isn't meant to stay with just one person—not only can it be used as a tool for learning from the past in order to help shape the future, but it can also be used to connect with one another. And if you're socially awkward at parties like me, sometimes trivia was the only thing I felt comfortable talking about.

When Moxie started her podcast, I was intimidated by her. I had already been doing *The Story Behind* for a while, and I didn't know many other hosts in the trivia and fun facts area, and certainly not a lot of females.

I also began to realize I was not the trivia buff I thought I was. I liked it and could research it, but Moxie ate, breathed, and slept trivia. She was the trivia podcast host I *wanted* to be, to be honest.

You would think that would make us "competitors," but that's not quite how podcasting works. I happily listened to her show, I got to know her online, shared her and her show with my audience, and roomed with her at a podcasting conference. I liked her instantly. She's a weird human, just like me. Probably just like you, if you bought this book.

So, hello, fellow, weird human! If you are hungry for trivia and fun facts, I know you'll enjoy feeding your curiosity with *Your Brain on Facts*, as I have.

—Emily Prokop, author of *The Story Behind* and host of *The Story Behind* podcast

INTRODUCTION

•

Why are we here? Not philosophically, but why are you hearing a voice in your head that corresponds to the lines and shapes I arranged in a Word document some months prior? We're here because your teachers lied to you. They didn't mean to. They did the best they could with the information they had, and goodness knows they work hard. Our history textbooks are riddled with highly believable misinformation called "cemented apocrypha" (by me, just now). By "cemented apocrypha," I mean stories that have become fact: Columbus was trying to prove the world was round; George Washington could not lie about cutting down a cherry tree; Paul Revere single-handedly rallied the colonial troops; Napoleon was short and bitter about it. Some version of the story was published in a book, then got copied to other books, and before long, it was the only version going. Thus we weren't taught that people already knew the world was round (Columbus, the annihilator of the people he discovered, thought Earth was smaller than scholars did); the cherry tree story first appeared in the fifth edition of a biography of George Washington (which left out Washington spending money lavishly while his troops starved in the snow); Revere wasn't the only rider (and he never finished the famous ride); Napoleon was a little above the average height for his time (and was both a ruthless dictator and a champion of gender-equal public education).

I've always loved facts, be they funny, practical, or outright weird. That led to an appetite for "the real story behind" explanations. I know I'm not alone in this. Otherwise, no one would be watching *Bill Nye: The Science Guy* or *Modern Marvels*, National Geographic wouldn't have its own channel, and no one would turn out for TED Talks. A love of knowledge isn't the shameful trait it was when I was in school in the 1980s–90s. In fact, being a nerd went beyond being acceptable and to being co-opted as fashion. That created a perfect climate to surreptitiously educate people who would not have cared otherwise, to kindle their innate curiosity.

A fine selection of books, documentaries, YouTube channels, and trivia games filled my brain to overflowing. Facts would fall out. Not fall, leap! Unsolicited bits of information would jump out of my mouth unbidden in any and all situations. Customers at the grocery store where I worked didn't want to hear that avocados have huge pits because the pits used to be distributed by giant sloths, and they definitely didn't want to hear about the human suffering inherent to cashew production. I once befuddled a heated online argument by explaining the history of the phrase "Devil's advocate" after someone used it. Trying to get through serious situations like traffic stops and funerals without dropping a few fact bombs is an agonizing struggle. Keeping my mouth shut and staying on-topic is like sprinting up six flights of stairs in high heels— exhausting and pretty much guaranteed to fail.

For the sake of everyone around me, I sought a safe way to vent all that cranial clutter. This was about the same time my husband turned me on to podcasts. More accurately, it was the time I finally relented to his efforts to get me to listen to a podcast. Prior to that, I didn't know how people found something they liked, I worried I would be bored, and I had the ridiculous but surprisingly common misapprehension that I had to stop everything I was doing to listen. Once I tried it, I was hooked, subscribing to entertaining and educational shows by the dozen. Facts were flowing into my ears like never before. It only took a hot minute before I decided that making a podcast would be the best way to divert the nonstop flow of facts, as well as to provide me with a creative outlet, now that I had retired from a seven-year stint as a burlesque dancer.

Thus was born the *Your Brain on Facts* podcast. The great thing about podcasting is that there's no barrier to entry, and anyone can do it. The downside of podcasting is that there is no barrier to entry, and anyone can do it. The first few episodes were rough because I wasn't editing enough. The next several were worse because I was editing and tweaking too much. Eventually, though, I got out of my own way so the audience could actually hear what I was saying. Topics ranged from the origins of blue raspberry to what will happen when Queen Elizabeth II dies, from children stolen by the government to prolific voice actors, from moral panics to Scandinavian Christmas monsters. The beginning of the podcast's second year saw me at a podcast conference several states away. Once I got over my first plane ride in twenty years, I found myself sharing a hotel room with a fellow fact-caster, Emily Prokop of *The Story Behind*. We got on like a house on fire, and a few shared cat videos later, Emily kindly put me on to her publisher.

It was time to write a book. One major hurdle in my research was that, as a rule, it was white men all the way down. History? White men from Julius Caesar to Boris Johnson. Medicine? White men from Hippocrates to Dr. Drew. Literature? White men from Shakespeare to George R. R. Martin. The stories of women, LGBT people, and people of color have been relegated to the edge of our sphere. Every time a white male story gets repeated, a female, queer, or POC story gets pushed a little further away. White men made up 90 percent of the textbooks our schools gave us. To do my small part to correct this, I tried to turn the focus of the articles you're about to read away from the "obvious" choices and toward the people whose stories aren't often told.

The world is a buffet of knowledge, an all-you-can-eat smorgasbord of information, especially in the age of Google. Unfortunately, this buffet has no sneeze guard, and sometimes the information gets befouled. Things get copied wrong, sources aren't cited, and internet trolls deliberately mislead and obfuscate. Pains were taken to corroborate the facts in this book. If I found something that was interesting enough to be included, it had to be from a respectable source or be found from at least two sources that didn't set off alarms of incredulity (or two sources that were not a flat-out copy and paste of one another, which happened even more than I'd expected).

I hope that this book fills your brain with new information, and that the facts contained herein ignite a curiosity in you to learn more. Don't under-value your local library. It's still one of the best places to grow a healthy mind.

Smorgasbord traditionally meant a small selection of breads and cheeses as an appetizer course. Meats, both hot and cold, were added over time and by the early twentieth century had come to be the main course.

CHAPTER 1

Science & Medicine

WHAT'S IN A (SCIENTIFIC) NAME?

From a lone example of a trilobite in Hunan, China named *Han solo* to a butterfly pea flower, reminiscent of a Georgia O'Keefe painting, called *Clitoria ternatea*, the naming of species offers almost as much in the way of entertainment as it does scientific classification. The animals we call by a single name, like horses, actually have a two-part name, *Equus caballas*. The official rules for naming species, set down by the International Commission on Zoological Nomenclature, are surprisingly simple. Scientific names must be spelled with the Latin alphabet and cannot be overtly offensive. That's basically it. The name can even be a nonsense string of arbitrary letters. In contrast, the naming of astronomical bodies (planets, stars, asteroids, etc.) is overseen by committees in accordance with strict naming conventions. While there is an enormous wealth of fascinating names to report on, from plants to drugs to telescopes, we'll confine ourselves to animals this time.

For as long as we have had records, and probably longer, mankind has sought to classify the world around us in an effort to understand it. This is called taxonomy, the study of the general principles of scientific classification, from the Greek words for "order" or "arrangement" and "science." Three centuries before the common era, Aristotle grouped animals first by similarities, like where they live, and then hierarchically, with humans naturally at the top. Not every animal fit well into that system. Ducks posed a particular problem, as they had an annoying habit of living in water, on the land, and spending time in the air. It would be 1800 years before another "natural philosopher," as scientists were called, would try his hand—Andrea Cesalpino, an Italian physician and botanist, sorted plants by the structure of their fruits and seeds. The first scientist to use a binomial, or two-name, system that we would recognize was Swiss botanist Gaspard Bauhin, who grouped some six thousand plants by genus and species in 1623.

There were several inconsistent and sometimes conflicting systems of classification in use when Carl Linnaeus wrote his influential *Systema Naturae* in 1735, laying down the system we use to this day. Linnaeus was the first taxonomist to list humans as a primate, though he did also classify whales as fish. All living things were sorted into kingdom, phylum, class, order, family, genus, species. A house cat, for example, is in kingdom Animalia, phylum Chordata (meaning it has a spinal cord), class Mammalia, order Carnivora, family Felidae, genus *Felis*, and species *catus*. A lion diverges from a house cat at genus *Panthera* (which awesomely means "reaper of all"); its species *leo* gives it the scientific name *Panthera leo*. This system can be visualized as an enormous branching tree, with its trunk being broad and its branches becoming increasingly specific.

We still name some animals according to their appearance, with a little poetic license thrown in for good measure. The tiniest and most pastel of the armored mammals is the pink fairy armadillo. As advertised, the star-nosed mole has a burst of delicate sensory tendrils on the tip of its snout. *Osexax mucofloris* is an unappealing worm who lives off the bones of dead whales, which would explain its name "bone-eating snot-flower." A bacterium that was taken to the international space station and exposed to cosmic radiation earned the Latin name for "traveler of the void." Central and Eastern areas of the US boast a salamander species that can grow to a whopping two and a half feet long called the hellbender. The internet's favorite ichthus, which can't maintain its body shape out of water and collapses into a rather dour-looking puddle, is the blob fish.

Even with the Linnaean taxonomy in place, we still call some animals things that they simply are not. We all know that a seahorse isn't a horse and koala bears aren't bears, but most people don't realize that a jackrabbit isn't a rabbit but a hare. Both animals come from the Leporidae family, but part ways when it comes to genus. Hares tend to live alone and not in burrows, and their young are born sighted with full coats of fur. Jackrabbits get their name from have exceptionally long ears, like a donkey or jackass. If you have ever found yourself watching *Go! Diego, Go!* after your preschooler has left the room, you've probably seen the lanky maned wolf. It should come as no surprise that this awkward-looking creature isn't from the genus *Canis*, like gray wolves, jackals, and dogs, but has the genus *Chrysocyon* all to itself. Red pandas are pandas, but giant pandas are not. Take a moment with that one. The adorable raccoon-like *Ailurus fulgens* were the first to be called "panda," which is believed to derive from the Nepali word *ponya*. When the black and white *Ailuropoda melanoleuca* were discovered later, it was assumed that the two species were related, so they were dubbed "giant pandas." They are from the family Ursidae, which includes all bears, but the giant panda is the only living species in its genus. What Americans call a buffalo is actually a bison by genus, whereas the cape buffalo from Africa and the water buffalo from Asia are not even in the same genus as each other.

The slimy hellbender.

Never let it be said that scientists have no sense of humor. Slime mold is the primary food for a beetle discovered in 2004, so their genus was labeled *Gelae*, pronounced "jelly." The species are *Gelae baen*, *Gelae belae*, *Gelae donut*, *Gelae fish*, and *Gelae rol*. There are beetles of the *Agra* genus named *Agra phobia* and *Agra vation*. There's a wasp whose genus is *Heerz* and species is *lukenatcha*. A species of tiny mollusk is called *ittibitium*, a parrot is named *Vini vidivici*, a water beetle is *Ytu brutus*, a syrphid fly is called *Ohmyia omya*, and there is the Pacific island snail *Ba humbugi*.

Scientists are more than the stereotype of stuffy old men in thick glasses and lab coats, poring over dry data sets. They're people, with interests and hobbies outside their work. When arachnologist Peter Jager discovered a new species of spider in Malaysia that was covered with flamboyant red, orange, and yellow hair, he could think of no better name than *Heteropoda davidbowie*. A frog, two types of flies, and an isopod found near Zanzibar have been named after Freddie Mercury. A species of horsefly with a conspicuous hind end was name *Scaptia beyonceae*. Likewise, a mustache-shaped pattern on a Cameroonian spider earned it the name *Pachygnatha zappa*, after rock legend Frank Zappa. The pistol shrimp *Synalpheus pinkfloydi* makes a noise louder than a rock concert at over two hundred decibels, simply by snapping its one oversized claw shut. The gall wasps have left the building, at least if they are the variety *Preseucoila imallshookupis*. The wasp *Metallichneumon neurospastarchus*'s genus honors the band Metallica while its species, *neurospastarchus*, Greek for "master of puppets," alludes to the weak and mindless nature of its hosts.

The pistol shrimp.

Actors get naming nods, too. Dominic Monaghan has a one-centimeter ginger spider named for him, *Ctenus monaghani*, after it was discovered during the filming of the nature documentary he hosted, *Wild Things*. After "shamelessly begging on national television" to have something named after him, late-night host and satirist, Stephen Colbert became namesake to a dune-dwelling spider in Southern California, *Aptostichus stephencolberti*. A fluffy lemur on the island of Madagascar shares its name with fierce creature and Monty Python John Cleese, *Avahi cleesei*. The hosts of *Top Gear* each have a wasp in the genus *Kerevata* named after them: *clarksoni*, *hammondi*, and *jamesmayi*.

Former First Lady of Argentina and well-traveled corpse Eva Peron has a moth named for her whose scientific name is simply *evita*. A single genus of fish honors Bill Clinton, Al Gore, Jimmy Carter, and Teddy Roosevelt. The neck plate of a leaf-dwelling Madagascan praying mantis earned it the name *Ilomantis ginsburgae*, in honor of Supreme Court Justice Ruth Bader Ginsburg. Sirindhorn, the second daughter of the monarch of Thailand, commonly referred to as "princess angel" has been honored with a number of plants, several crustaceans, a butterfly, a bee, and a prehistoric tarsier. Similarly, Barack Obama's name was stamped on several spider species, a few different fish, a blood fluke, bird, lichen, beetle, extinct reptile, horsehair worm, and a bee. He and wife Michelle were dually honored with the fish *Teleogramma obamaorum*.

Terry Pratchett, whose Discworld books described the world as resting on the back of a giant turtle, is the namesake of the turtle species *Psephophorus terrypratchetti*. Shakespeare has a wasp named for him, while Henry David Thoreau has two. The author of *Gulliver's Travels*, Jonathan Swift, is the namesake of a fly that's naturally quite tiny, while Herman Melville's name was given to a whale. Gene Roddenberry has a true bug, Arthur C. Clarke has a dinosaur, Neil Gaiman has a beetle, and H.P. Lovecraft has a wasp. An extinct crab was named for Ray Harryhausen, the man who brought stop-motion movie monsters to life. J. R. R. Tolkien has gotten a great deal of scientific love, in the form of a beetle, a crustacean, two wasps, and a clam. In addition to the false-headed moth *Erechthias beeblebroxi*, *Hitchhiker's Guide to the Galaxy* author Douglas Adams has an ant named for himself and a triple-finned fish named after a character, *Fiordichthys slartibartfasti*.

Jonathan Swift, the author, not the fly.

It should go without saying that there is great overlap between the lovers of science and the lovers of science fiction and all things geeky. Tolkien appears again with a shark named for Gollum, a cyclopic shark named for Sauron, an ancient croc called *balrogus*, and an entire genus of cordylid lizards name *Smaug*. A tiny armored catfish from South America was christened *Otocinclus batmani*; no word on if it fights crime at night. Harry Potter fans will want to steer clear of the *Ampulex dementor* wasp, which turns cockroaches into zombies. Science has given us *Spongiforma squarepantsii*, but it's not a sponge, it's a highly porous mushroom. A trilobite that reminded the discoverer of the faces of the two old curmudgeons in the Muppet Theater box was dubbed *Geragnostus waldorfstatleri*. A newly discovered genus of wasp has each of its species named for a different house in Game of Thrones: *Laelius arryni, baratheoni, lannisteri, martelli, targaryeni, tullyi,* and *starki.*

Scientists not only honored cartoonist Gary Larson with the scientific name of a chewing louse that feeds on owls, they also borrowed a name from him. A 1982 *Far Side* cartoon showed a caveman leading a lecture on the dangers of dinosaurs, pointing to a slide of a stegosaurus's spiked tail and saying, "Now this end is called the thagomizer, after the late Thag Simmons." The term became an informal but widely used anatomical term, being used by the likes of the Smithsonian and the BBC. And no, they don't care that humans and stegosauri lived sixty million years apart, and neither do we.

Sometimes, scientists plain run out of ideas. After finding nine other species of cicada-like leafhopper, their discoverer dubbed the next one he found *Erythroneura ix*, or nine in Roman numerals. Another scientist found so many species of olethreutid moths that he eventually opted for an alphabetical ascension to come up with names, i.e. *Eucosma bobana, e. cocana, e. dodana, e. fofana*, and so on.

LOVE HURTS

Dating sucks and 41 percent of first marriages end in divorce, but humans have it easy compared to many things that walk, swim, slither, or fly. If you worry about losing your sense of self in a relationship, be grateful you are not an angler fish. "Angler fish" refers broadly to those slightly horrifying aquatic creatures with as much mouth as body, who lure their prey in with wormy or glowing bits of flesh at the end of an antenna-like appendage. When nineteenth century scientists began to catalog the members of the suborder Ceratioidei, which contains such pleasantly named creatures as sea devils, devilfish, and deep-sea anglerfish, all the specimens they could find were female, and scientists had no idea what the males even looked like. They sometimes found fish that seemed to be related, but they were much smaller and lacked the frightening jaws and lure typical of ceratioids, so they were placed into different taxonomic groups. In 1922, almost a full century after the first ceratioid was recorded, an Icelandic biologist discovered a female ceratioid with two of these smaller fish with their faces attached to her body, which he assumed was a mother and her babies in a puzzling configuration. An ichthyologist at the British Museum of Natural History also found a smaller fish attached to a female ceratioid. When he dissected it, it became clear that the smaller fish was not the larger fish's offspring; it was her mate.

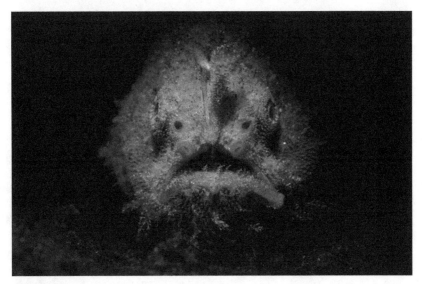

She'll take care of you.

Scientists soon figured out why the "missing" male ceratioids looked so different. They aren't built to hunt and devour prey because they don't hunt. They nourish themselves by attaching to a female. Male angler fish are parasites as much as they are mates. A male ceratioid finds his mate by following species-specific pheromones to a female. The female will guide the males in by flashing her bio-luminescent lure, like a ground crew waving on an airplane with their orange flashlights. Once the male reaches her, he bites into the female's abdomen and latches on. His body then fuses with hers. They now share a circulatory system, which allows the male to get the nutrients he needs from the female's blood. Since the male has no further need of eyes for seeing or fins for swimming, those body parts(and others including organs) wither away. The relationship isn't completely one-sided, though. While the male is taking blood, he also provides sperm when the female is ready to spawn.

Got You Under My Skin

On your next Mediterranean holiday, go for a dive and see if you can spot something that looks like a sausage casing full of green gelatin undulating gracefully in the water. That is a female *Bonellia viridis*, the green spoon worm. You will know you are looking at a female because only they have the bright green coloration and because the two-millimeter long male *Bonellia viridis* are more likely to be found inside the female.

> The largest penis relative to body size in the animal kingdom belongs to the barnacle at ten times the length of its body. The smallest relative penis belongs to the gorilla. A four hundred pound (or 181 kilogram) adult male gorilla has a penis only two inches (or five centimeters) when erect.

Green spoon worms can determine the sex of other green spoon worms. They begin life as genderless larvae, drifting on the ocean current. If the larva lands on a bit of ocean floor not currently claimed by an adult green spoon worm, it will develop into a female and begin secreting a toxin called bonellin. Bonellin makes the adult green spoon worms green but has an even more dramatic effect on their larvae. If a larva comes in contact with the bonellin toxin, it will turn into a male. The female then sucks the newly made male into her body through her feeding proboscis. He now exists for the sole purpose of providing the female with sperm. It's a one-way trip for the male, but at least he won't be alone. A few dozen males may find themselves living in a chamber in the female's body where they absorb nutrients from the fluid they are bathed in. Like the male anglerfish, male green spoon worms exist to provide sperm, so they only need the organs associated with that task and have few organs otherwise.

Use It and Maybe Lose It

You may think there are no more boring animals in the world than slugs, but mollusk mating is action-packed. Take for instance the mascot of UC Santa Cruz, the banana slug. Like all snails and slugs, banana slugs are hermaphrodites, possessing both male and female sex organs. Things are evenly matched when banana slugs mate—each slug produces eggs and each one has a penis. Their penis can grow to be longer than their body, hence the species name, *dolichophallus*, or "long penis." Mating starts off a bit rough, with the slugs striking at each other like snakes and even taking bites out of one another. Then, they arrange themselves head-to-tail, like a yellow yin-yang, and achieve intromission. Mating can last for hours, during which the slugs may exchange sperm and fertilize each other's eggs equally, or one may fertilize the other. Breaking up can be hard to do, especially when one slug's penis gets stuck in its partner. If mutual thrashing around can't dislodge it, the other slug may chew the offending member off. This apophallation ("penis removal" for non-limacologists) renders the slug female, as penises don't regenerate.

Go, Santa Cruz!

Being female is more resource-demanding than being male, what with having to nourish and support eggs. Most animals have no choice but to accept their assigned role. Flatworms, however, take a proactive approach to avoiding motherhood by trying to stab the other with their penis in an act called "penis fencing." When two potential mates meet, they rear up, which makes room for them to strike with their two-headed penis on the offense, but defensively leaves their body vulnerable. Penis fencing can last an hour, with the flatworms being stabbed multiple times, until one manages to deposit sperm into the other. The victor swims away, his paternal duties complete. The losing flatworm begins to search for the extra food required for making eggs. Flatworms practice "traumatic insemination" and they are not the only ones. Bedbugs, thorny-headed worms, microscopic roundworms, wheel animalcules, fruit flies, sea slugs, and spiders in the genus *Harpactea* also prefer to go through their mate's abdomen rather than through their genital tract.

Firm Handshake

The argonaut, or paper nautilus, is a small octopus found in the open ocean. Argonauts are one of the most sexually dimorphic octopodes, meaning the females are considerably larger than the males, about eight times larger and six hundred times heavier. The females secrete a thin, white, brittle shell, which had been thought for centuries to be for egg storage. More recently, argonauts have been observed using their shells to trap air from the surface so they will be neutrally buoyant at their preferred depth. Like many octopodes, the male argonaut's third left arm develops into a hectocotylus, the cephalopod version of a penis, which the male can detach for copulation. What makes the argonaut's hectocotylus different is that, once detached, it can swim over to the female on its own, where it attaches itself inside her pallial cavity (octopus vagina). One mark in the "pro" column for this approach is that the male argonaut can pass on his genetic information while staying a safe distance from the larger female so that he does not become part of her egg-nourishing meal plan. The hectocotylus regenerates, so he who mates and runs away may live to mate another day.

Gender Roles

Males typically benefit from mating as much as possible, in part because they can, while the females, who actually raise the offspring, have to be choosy about their partners. In a cave in Brazil lives a species of tiny louse who did not get the memo. For *Neotrogla curvata*, females seek out multiple mates and the males are the choosier sex. Also, the female has a penis, and the male has the equivalent of a vagina, so they did not get that memo, either. There are four species of tiny three-millimeter *Neotrogla*, and the females all have penises.

During mating sessions that can last for two to three nonstop days, the female penetrates the male and uses her genitals to collect sperm rather than deliver it. The female's erect, curved protrusion is called a gynosome. During sex, the male still ejaculates, but inside his own body instead of hers. When the female penetrates the male, he delivers sperm into a duct in her gynosome, which leads to a storage organ. Because *Neotrogla* sex is a marathon, the mating pair have to anchor themselves. The female inflates the base of her gynosome, which is covered with tiny spines, inside the male, and it's impossible to separate a mating pair without killing the male.

The multi-national team that discovered the *Neotrogla* won the Ig Nobel Prize for biology in 2017 for their paper, *Female Penis, Male Vagina, and Their Correlated Evolution in a Cave Insect.*

Who Runs the World?

Shaking up traditional gender roles isn't exclusive to insects but can also be seen in the committee-assembled critter that is the spotted hyena. Unlike with most mammals, the top tier of the social order is held by females, by dint of being significantly more muscular and aggressive than the males. Males rank below all the females and even the cubs. Their social standing can only change if a male above them dies or if another male joins their pack, as the newbie is automatically assigned the lowest rank, but they can never rise above the females. Female spotted hyenas are so masculine that they develop a pseudo-penis, complete with false testicles and scrotum, which makes them notoriously difficult for researchers to sex, even when the animal is tranquilized. This unique genital transformation comes from a prenatal infusion of androgen, a male sex hormone. Not every female gets the same hormone boost, though.

Researchers in Kenya who studied the spotted hyena for nearly two decades discovered that high-ranking females give their fetal pups higher levels of androgen in the final stages of pregnancy than lower-ranking females do. This means that the mother's rank in the pack could directly affect her offspring's physical traits beyond what her genes do. In packs of forty or more individuals who scavenge to survive, aggressiveness and muscle mass are good traits to have. The extra androgen helps increases the likelihood that the genes of a more aggressive female will survive. It comes at a cost, though. The androgen that the fetal females receive damages their ovaries, making it more difficult to conceive when they are mature. The androgen is also what causes the female spotted hyena's genitals to change, a lot. The clitoris elongates to protrude anywhere from seven to twenty-three inches (or eighteen to fifty-eight centimeters) from her body, hanging down from her belly like a male penis. The only visual difference between the pseudo-penis and an actual penis is the shape of the tip—blunt on females and pointed on males. This pseudo-penis can become erect and female hyenas even urinate through them. The spotted hyena clitoris isn't the same as the clitoris of a human; theirs also contains the birth canal.

Mating is a complex cluster of social protocol and acrobatics. Sex can only happen if the female retracts her pseudo-penis, meaning there is no way for a male to forcefully copulate, even if he somehow managed to physically overcome the female. In what is likely nature's way of encouraging genetic diversity, female spotted hyenas almost exclusively choose males who have joined their pack from another pack. Her estrus, or "heat," only lasts about three days, though female spotted hyenas show no outward signs, at least as far as human researchers can tell.

The female spotted hyena chooses her mate, then leads or chases the smaller male to a secluded spot. She needs safety more than privacy. Research on captive hyenas at the University of California, Berkeley, has shown that the glans of the male's penis swells in the female's reproductive tract after the male ejaculates, causing a "copulatory lock," as happens with domestic dogs. This leaves the mating couple vulnerable to larger predators like lions, so, as in real estate, spotted hyena mating is all about location, location, location.

The female spotted hyena then stands still and lowers her head, her way of saying, "I promise I won't bite you, for a few minutes...probably." Cooperation only goes so far; the male still has the comparatively tricky task of getting his penis into the opening of the female's retracted pseudo-penis. Careful positioning is required for the male to crouch behind her and, with a bit of hopping, somehow get his penis to point up and backward to enter her clitoris. It takes time and practice to get it right, and the inexperienced male can try the female's patience.

As hard as mating might be for the male spotted hyena, the real difficulty comes four months later for the female. She must delivery her cubs, usually two or three in a litter, through her pseudo-penis. The birth canal is only about an inch in diameter and squeezing a two-pound cub through this narrow opening can result in significant tearing. It's not uncommon for cubs to become trapped and die, tearing or no tearing. This often leads to the mother's death as well. Between bleeding, infection, and the complications of trapped cubs, maternal mortality rates in spotted hyenas hover around 60 percent. For those who survive, things get a little easier as the resulting scar will actually stretch more than the surrounding tissue during the next delivery.

But the babies sure are cute!

PHYSICIAN, TEST THYSELF

When you want something done right, you have to do it yourself. This philosophy is okay when it comes to loading the dishwasher, but maybe not when you are trying find the cause of venereal disease. No one told that to John Hunter. Medical types in the eighteenth century medical believed gonorrhea and syphilis were caused by the same pathogen. Hunter injected himself with gonorrhea to test the theory. He contracted gonorrhea *and* syphilis, most likely from using the same needle to get the samples. His is just one of many sometimes-harrowing stories of doctors and scientists using themselves as test subjects.

Isaac Newton. That wig is *working*.

Better than a Poke in the Eye

Let's start with one of the OGs of science, Isaac Newton. Newton had many areas of interest beyond fruit-based physics. For the sake of science, Newton stuck a needle in his eye. He thought that if he slid a long needle called a bodkin between his eyeball and eye socket, his vision would change. It did! He saw different colors and dots of light that appeared when he applied pressure. It's the same lights that you see if you press on your eyes, called phosphenes. Newton also stared at the sun in a mirror, repeatedly, until the image of the sun stayed when he closed his eye. It stayed for months, in fact. He had to spend three days in a dark room until it faded enough for him to resume his daily life.

Huff-rey Davies

While at the Medical Pneumatic Institute of Bristol in the 1790s, Humphrey Davy studied gases. Studied by inhaling, in case the theme of this section was still in any way unclear. Davy would set up chemical reactions and inhale the resulting gas. One gas gave him a pleasant sensation and impulse to laugh at everything; he had discovered nitrous oxide, a.k.a. laughing gas. Though his efforts were meant to reproduce the pleasurable effects of things like alcohol and opium, Davy would ultimately recommend nitrous oxide for use as an anesthetic. Modern dentists use a blend of 50 percent nitrous and 50 percent oxygen, but Davy was huffing 100 percent nitrous, which is probably why he enjoyed it enough to start hosting parties where friends would inhale it from silk bags.

"Could You Patent the Sun?"

When it came time to test his polio vaccine, Dr. Jonas Salk decided the only suitable test subject was himself...and his family. In 1947, Salk was working on a vaccine for the crippling disease at the University of Pittsburgh. He needed a healthy volunteer to test it, and administered it to himself, his wife, and their three sons. It worked and the vaccine was soon tested nationwide and showed dramatic results. In two years, cases of polio decreased from about 29,000 to 6,000. Salk did not patent the vaccine and insisted that it remain free and available to everyone. Thus, he is often remembered as one of history's great humanitarians.

Heart of the Matter

In 1921, Werner Forssmann was a German urologist who pioneered the technique of cardiac catheterization—the insertion of a catheter into the heart to measure the pressure inside to help determine if a patient needs surgery. Inspired by the work of scientists who had catheterized a horse in 1861, Forssmann wanted to test catheterization in humans but could not get permission for such a dangerous-sounding experiment. Deciding to take a different tack, he asked an operating room nurse to set up the necessary equipment and assist him. She agreed, but only on the noble condition that he perform the procedure on her rather than trying to experiment on himself. No sooner was the nurse prepped on the table than Forssmann anesthetized his own arm and made a cut, inserting the catheter twelve inches (or thirty centimeters) into his vein. He then calmly climbed two flights of stairs to the x-ray suite before threading it the rest of the way into his heart and getting an x-ray to check the placement. He was later forced to resign from that hospital, then hired back, then fired again.

Great Balls of Science

In the early '30s, Doctors Herbert Woollard and Edward Carmichael observed that patients sometimes experienced pain in unrelated parts of their body when an internal organ was damaged. To learn more about that phenomenon, they decided to deliberately damage one of their own organs. But what organs were both noncritical and easily damaged? Perhaps an organ, or a pair of organs, that were outside the body. Yes, they *chose* to experiment with their gentlemen's bits to study pain. In their notes, Woollard and Carmichael recorded that "the testis was drawn forward" and placed under a pan, though they did not note whose testis nor who did the drawing forward. They then added weights to the pan and recorded the resulting sensations. The pair performed the experiment multiple times, eventually concluding that testicular pain often came with generalized torso pain. If only one testicle was harmed, only one side of the torso would feel its effects. Was their bravery worth it? Doctors still note the "referred pain" that comes along with testicular trauma, so they helped advance medical knowledge in their own way.

After chemist Albert Hoffman first synthesized lysergic acid diethylamide (LSD) in 1941, he famously rode his bicycle home while under the influence of the drug. The date, April 19, became a pseudo-holiday in recreational pharmaceutical circles, called Bicycle Day.

Skin Deep

What would it take for you to willingly let parasitic hookworms burrow through your skin, live in your intestines, and feed off your blood? That's precisely what immunologist and biologist David Pritchard did in 2004. Auto-immune diseases like asthma and Crohn's disease are relatively uncommon in areas where hookworms are prevalent. Pritchard had a hypothesis that hookworm infections reduce allergy and asthma symptoms by modifying the body's immune response, but he needed human subjects to test. In order to appease his ethics committee, he agreed to be the guinea pig, along with volunteers from his team. "They itch quite a bit when they go through the skin," said Pritchard, but they became truly troublesome when they reached his stomach, causing pain and diarrhea. Fifty hookworms turned out to be too many; ten hookworms was a better number. The experiment later allowed for wider testing on humans, who reported miraculous relief of allergy symptoms. As of the date of publication, clinical trials are underway to evaluate hookworms as a treatment for various conditions, including multiple sclerosis.

Slapstick for Science

In 1898, German surgeon August Bier figured out that a dose of cocaine injected into the spinal fluid could serve as an effective anesthesia. In order to prove it this, he had his assistant, Augustus Hildebrandt, attempt to inject him, but Hildebrandt messed it up and Bier ended up leaking spinal fluid from a hole is his neck. Rather than abandon the experiment, the two men traded places. The injection went correctly this time. Bier proceeded to hit, stab, hammer, and even burn his assistant. He also pulled Hildebrandt's pubic hair and squashed his testicles. Both men suffered terribly for days after the cocaine wore off and they were able to feel pain again. While Bier took time off work to recover, Hildebrandt had to fill in for Bier. Perhaps unsurprisingly, Hildebrandt subsequently fell out with Bier, becoming one of his fiercest critics.

Sick Burn, Bro

In front of a full house at the Royal Institution in the United Kingdom in June 1903, physicist Pierre Curie, husband of two-time Nobel Prize winner Marie, displayed a burn on his arm caused by radium salts, which he had taped to his arm for ten hours more than fifty days prior. During the demonstration, Curie dropped some radium on the desk. The resulting contamination was still detectable half a century later. The Curies hoped that radium's burning effect might prove useful in the treatment of cancer. Ironically, the radiation from that the sample, as well as other chemicals the Curies routinely exposed themselves to, had a catastrophic effect on their health. Both Pierre and Marie persevered though constant sickness, fatigue, and pain to continue their experiments, which set the course for the use of radium in medicine.

The Ffirth and Hopefully Last

A special place in science heaven must be reserved for Stubbins Ffirth, who, as a medical student in the early nineteenth century, conducted a series of potentially lifesaving but definitely stomach-turning experiments to prove that yellow fever was not contagious. Yellow fever is a viral disease that causes fever, chills, loss of appetite, nausea, muscle pains, and headaches, and can be fatal. At the time, doctors believed yellow fever passed from person to person, like the flu, but Ffirth disagreed. He began by taking "fresh black vomit" from a yellow fever patient and pouring it onto cuts in his arm. He did not come down with yellow fever. Emboldened, Ffirth collected a patient's vomit and put it in his eyes. He smeared himself with all manner of bodily fluids, including blood, saliva, sweat, and urine. He sat in a "vomit sauna," an enclosed space full of heated vomit fumes, which caused him "great pain in [his] head," but did not otherwise affect his health. Finally, he took to eating the vomit, first in pill form, then straight from a patient's mouth. Satisfied with his thoroughness, Ffirth published his 1804 book *A Treatise on Malignant Fever; with an Attempt to Prove Its Non-Contagious Nature*, in which he declared categorically that yellow fever not contagious. Yellow fever *is* in fact contagious, but only through blood transmission via mosquito bite. This was proven by another self-experimenter, US Army surgeon Jesse Lazear, a century later, when he allowed himself to be bitten by mosquitoes carrying yellow fever. Lazear would ultimately die of a mosquito-borne disease, not from one of the mosquitoes he bred for his experiments, but from a wild mosquito who happened by.

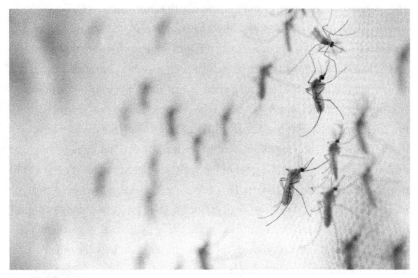

These ladies are the worst.

Giving Me Agita

Just as Ffirth swam against the tide of yellow fever contagion, Dr. Barry Marshall was sure the medical establishment had the wrong idea about stomach ulcers. The accepted wisdom was that stomach ulcers were the result of stress and other lifestyle factors, but Marshall was sure the culprit was the *Helicobacter pylori* bacterium. To prove his hypothesis, Marshall and pathologist Robin Warren needed to examine the bacteria in a human body, but as Marshall explained to *New Scientist* in a 2006 interview, "I was the only person informed enough to consent." Marshall did not tell his hospital's ethics committee what he planned until after he had swallowed the bacteria. He did not even tell his wife. The first three days were unremarkable, then Marshall began vomiting; his wife complained that he had "putrid breath." A biopsy at the two-week mark confirmed that he had gastritis, which can lead to ulcers. While it took some years for Marshall and Warren's theory to gain traction, they were awarded the 2005 Nobel Prize for Physiology or Medicine.

Australia: Satan's Aquarium

A jellyfish was to Queensland doctor Jack Barnes what *Helicobacter pylori* was to Marshall. A strange illness, now called Irukandji syndrome, had appeared in Australia in the mid-twentieth century, characterized by severe muscle aches, nausea, and blinding pain. It also had a truly bizarre symptom—patients would experience levels of anxiety so severe that some asked their doctors to kill them. The cause was unknown, but it seemed to come from the sea, as most patients had been swimming prior to the onset of symptoms. Barnes winnowed down the possible causes to a species of tiny, nearly transparent box jellyfish. To test this theory, the doctor stung himself with the tentacle of the *Carukia barnesi*. He was not alone, though. Probably losing his shot at "father of the year," he also stung his nine-year-old son, as well as a young lifeguard. (It's not documented how Barnes knew the lifeguard or how he talked the lifeguard into it.) Not long after being stung, all three had to be hospitalized for their excruciating pain. All three test subjects made complete recoveries, though there was no word on how the ordeal affected the Barnes' father-son dynamic.

Once Bitten...

If you have ever been stung by a bee, you probably called it "painful." If you have been bitten by a bullet ant, you might call it a "pure, intense, brilliant pain. Like walking over flaming charcoal with a three-inch nail embedded in your heel." Thankfully, you do not need to be bitten by a bullet ant, because biologist Justin Schmidt already has. Schmidt has let himself been stung and bitten by nearly a thousand painful creatures, taking careful notes along the way. He created the Schmidt Sting Pain Index, a way of quantifying and describing the pain that insects inflict, which is both elucidating and entertaining, in a schadenfreude kind of way. Schmidt ranked each insect sting on a rising scale of one to four and described each incident rather lyrically. The sting of the sweat bee registered a one on the pain scale and felt "Light and ephemeral. Almost fruity. A tiny spark has singed a single hair on your arm." Garnering a score of two, a yellowjacket's sting was described as being "hot and smoky, almost irreverent. Imagine W. C. Fields extinguishing a cigar on your tongue." At a three, the sting of the Maricopa harvester ant was described as "after eight unrelenting hours of drilling into that ingrown toenail, you find the drill wedged into the toe." The description of the warrior wasp sting, which scored a four and lasted for hours, showed Schmidt's realization of the absurdity of his bodily sacrifice: "Torture. You are chained in the flow of an active volcano. Why did I start this list?" The stand-out entry is the tarantula hawk, widely regarded as the most painful sting yet discovered by man: "Blinding, fierce, shockingly electric. A running hair dryer has been dropped into your bubble bath. A bolt out of the heavens. Lie down and scream."

The tarantula hawk. Stay away.

In the late 1990s, Kevin Warwick had a silicon chip transponder implanted into his forearm. According to his website, the neural interface allowed him to "operate doors, lights, heaters and other computers without lifting a finger." The experiment was called Project Cyborg.

Negative Findings

Not everyone got a shiny medal or professional acclaim for their self-experimentation. Some merely got maimed or killed. Scottish inventor, scientist, and writer Sir David Brewster, had a particular interest in optics and light polarization, a field of study which requires good eyesight. Unfortunately for Brewster, he performed a chemical experiment in 1831 which nearly blinded him. His vision returned, but he was plagued with eye troubles for the rest of his life. His legacy in vision did not result from any experiment, but from his invention, the kaleidoscope. Also in the sacrificing-sight-for-science club was Robert Bunsen, best known giving his name to the Bunsen burner (and an under-appreciated Muppet). He began his scientific career in organic chemistry, but nearly died twice of arsenic poisoning. Soon thereafter, he lost the sight in his right eye to an explosion of cacodyl cyanide. These being excellent reasons to change fields, Bunsen moved to inorganic chemistry, where he developed the field of spectroscopy, which measures and examines light and radiation.

See Right Through You

Elizabeth Fleischman Ascheim was not a doctor herself, but worked in the office of her brother-in-law, Dr. Michael J.H. Woolf. Woolf was intrigued by the new discovery of Wilhelm Conrad Röntgen: x-rays. Ascheim became equally interested and, with Woolf's encouragement, gave up her job as a bookkeeper to study electrical science. In 1897, she bought an x-ray machine, the first in San Francisco, which she moved into the office. The duo spent nine years experimenting with the machine, using themselves as subjects. The effects of long-term exposure to x-rays was not understood at the time, and their protective measures in place were inadequate. Ascheim died of widespread, aggressive cancer.

New Blood

It may have been the quest for eternal youth that led Russian physician, economist, and science fiction writer, Alexander Bogdanov to experiment with blood transfusion in 1924. After performing eleven transfusions on himself, he declared that his balding had stopped and his eyesight had improved. Unfortunately, Boganov had not screened the blood he was using for infectious diseases, leading him to transfuse himself with blood infected with malaria and tuberculosis, which killed him.

UNSUNG-EST HEROES OF MEDICINE

When you think of world-saving heroes, obvious answers come to mind: Superman, Captain America, Randy Quaid's character from *Independence Day*, the usual. But there are real life people who have saved thousands, millions, and arguably a billion lives in the real world, within living memory, and you probably never heard their names.

Maurice Hilleman

As someone who did not die as a child from a preventable disease, it is the author's considered opinion that vaccines are the bee's knees. Most of the vaccines that have kept us alive for the past two generations were created by one man, who did not even want credit for it. Eradicating childhood diseases through vaccination was the life work of virologist Maurice Hilleman. By the time of his death in 2005 at age eighty-five, he had developed vaccines for measles-mumps-rubella, chickenpox, meningitis, pneumonia, hepatitis A, hepatitis B, and dozens more.

The fragility of life was with Maurice Hilleman from the day he was born in 1919, when both his twin sister and mother died. This was the same year the Spanish flu killed around 5 percent of the world's population. After high school, Hilleman earned a full scholarship to Montana State University. Majoring in chemistry and microbiology, he graduated first in his class, going on to graduate school to earn his doctorate in microbiology from the University of Chicago in 1944.

When Hilleman started his first job at the pharmaceutical company E. R. Squibb & Sons in 1944, American soldiers deployed in Japan had been contracting Japanese encephalitis-B from infected mosquitoes. As chief of what is today the Walter Reed Army Institute of Research, Hilleman studied pandemics. He was able to recognize patterns in the type and severity of pandemics and could predict with stunning accuracy when they would hit. When Hilleman and a colleague saw signs of an impending flu pandemic spreading through Hong Kong in 1957, they raced against the clock to produce and distribute forty million vaccines. About 69,000 Americans died from that flu, but the toll would have been far worse without the vaccine.

American Samoa was one of the only places not to see a single Spanish flu death, because the governor took the reports he was hearing seriously and blocked all incoming ships from making port.

Can we all go to American Samoa now?

Hilleman moved to the Merck pharmaceutical company and continued his laser-focused attention on the prevention of other diseases. Some hit close to home. When his daughter Jeryl Lynn came down with the mumps in 1967, he swabbed her throat and collected the virus specimens to take back to his lab. His other daughter, one-year-old Kirsten, was among the first to take the experimental vaccine. "There was a baby being protected by a virus from her sister, and this has been unique in the history of medicine, I think," Hilleman remembered in an interview. The strain that Hilleman collected from his daughter reduced the incidence of mumps from 186,000 cases a year to fewer than 1,000 cases. For perspective, that's equivalent of reducing the capacity of Rose Bowl Stadium twice-over to half the capacity of a suburban high school.

In the early 1960s, measles killed more than five hundred American children annually. Hilleman and pediatrician Joseph Stokes found that they could minimize the side effects of the measles vaccine by giving a gamma globulin shot in one arm and the vaccine in the other, which helped to quell parental concerns and improve the rate of immunization. Hilleman continued to refine the vaccine, eventually producing the much safer strain that is still in use today. Rather than put his name on it, Hilleman named it "Moraten," short for "more attenuated enders." "Attenuated" means weakened, and much of the work had been done in John F. Enders' laboratory at Boston Children's Hospital.

In the spring of 1963, a rubella epidemic began in Europe and quickly swept around the globe. In the US alone, around 11,000 newborns died and 20,000 suffered birth defects, including deafness, heart disease, and cataracts. Hilleman was already testing a vaccine he had developed, but agreed to work with a vaccine from federal regulators, which he later described as "toxic, toxic, toxic." By 1969, he had cleaned it up enough to obtain FDA approval and prevent another rubella epidemic. In 1971, he combines the measles, mumps, and rubella vaccines to make the MMR vaccine, replacing a series of six shots with two.

In 1978, having found a better rubella vaccine than his own, Hilleman asked its developer if he could use it in the MMR. The developer, Dr. Stanley Plotkin of the Wistar Institute in Philadelphia, was speechless. It was an expensive choice for Hilleman's employer and might have been a painful one for anyone other than Dr. Hilleman. According to Plotkin, "It's not that he didn't have an ego. He certainly did, but he valued excellence above that. Once he decided that this strain was better, he did what he had to do," even if it meant sacrificing his work.

It's impossible to know how many lives Maurice Hilleman's work has saved. By one estimate, it is eight million *per year*. Though he was forced to retire at age sixty-five, he continued to work for the greater good, serving as an adviser to the World Health Organization. He never won a Nobel Prize, but Hilleman did receive the National Medal of Science from President Ronald Reagan in 1988.

Youyou Tu

When it comes to deadly animals, sharks, cobras, and anything native to Australia, all pale in comparison to the mosquito, courtesy of its tiny passenger, malaria. For example, in 2008, *plasmodia*, the parasite that causes malaria, infected 247 million people and caused almost one million deaths. Symptoms include fever, headache, and vomiting. Malaria can quickly become life-threatening by disrupting the blood supply to vital organs. The disease strikes children hard, especially in sub-Saharan Africa. Thanks in part to traveling humans, malaria affects more than a hundred countries, from Asia, Latin America, the Middle East, to parts of Europe.

The single greatest arrow in our quiver in the fight against malaria was discovered by a doctor looking not only to the future, but also to the wisdom of the past. The drug, called artemisinin, was found in the 1970s by Chinese scientist Youyou Tu and her team, who discovered ancient references to a fever-easing plant in traditional Chinese medical texts. Because of their work, malaria death rates have decreased 47 percent worldwide; the rate of infection in children has dropped 46 percent.

Tu was born in Zhejiang, China in 1930. A tuberculosis infection interrupted her high school education but inspired her to go into medical research. Tu graduated from Beijing Medical University School of Pharmacy in 1955 and attended the China Academy of Chinese Medical Sciences to continue her research on Chinese herbal medicine.

While teaching and researching in 1969, Tu was suddenly appointed head of a group of chemists and pharmacologists for a top-secret military program. Project 523 was established by Chairman Mao with the goal of finding ways to prevent and cure malaria. For two years, the project had focused on developing Western-style antimalarial drugs, but synthetic compounds bore no fruit, so Project 523 turned to traditional herbal medicine for answers. This was a surprising turn of events, considering one of Mao's objectives with the Cultural Revolution was to promote communist ideology by purging China of traditional literature and art. Because of this, scholars were considered the lowest caste of society, and scientific research was only sanctioned if the Communist Party decided the purpose was sufficiently practical. Tu was told she had been chosen because of her unique combination of skills—she had a degree in Western pharmacology, yet she could differentiate thousands of traditional herbs. Tu felt deeply honored to be appointed to the post, especially as a woman and relatively young, but she knew the task before her was a difficult one. Malaria can develop resistance to drugs faster than new ones can be created, and nearly a quarter-million compounds had already been tested by scientists around the world. Not making things any easier for Tu was the fact that her husband had been "sent down to the countryside" on a mandatory exchange program for "reeducation," leaving her a single parent; she would often be separated from her daughter for long periods of time.

Tu and her team traveled from village to village to talk to traditional medicine practitioners and scoured libraries for every medical text they could find. In the end, they collected over 2,000 recipes for herbal, animal, and mineral-based compounds, choosing from these 640 with the most potential. Back in Beijing, her team began distilling those best bets into 380 herbal extracts they could test on mice. One challenge was overcoming the primitive conditions of their own lab, which was poorly ventilated against the harsh solvents the team used and had only household pots and pans as equipment.

By 1971, the researched began to zero in on the herb *quinghao*, or sweet wormwood. It first appeared in a silk scroll from the Han Dynasty two thousand years ago entitled *Prescriptions for 52 Kinds of Diseases* and was mentioned frequently in texts throughout the centuries as a remedy for intermittent fevers, a symptom of malaria. That still left the team with many questions: Which species of *quinghao* did the texts refer to? Where did it grow? Which part of the plant do you use and how should it be prepared? Other research groups joined the quest and after an exacting process of elimination, *Artemisia annua L.* was found to be the only variety of *quinghao* containing antimalarial properties. Despite this, disappointingly, no extract of it had produced a consistent effect on the lab mice.

The miraculous sweet wormwood.

Frustrated, Tu began rereading the ancient texts, searching for clues. A medical manuscript from the East Jin Dynasty, written in 340 CE, advise, "A handful of *quinghao* immersed in two liters of water, wring out the juice, and drink it all." It was so simple! The team had been boiling samples and the heat had damaged the active ingredients. Tu immediately modified their methods and on October 4, 1971, they found a formulation that proved 100 percent effective in curing malaria-infected mice, though it would take an additional six years to isolate the drug's molecular structure. Tests in infected monkeys were also successful. The next step was testing humans. To move the process along as quickly as possible, Tu and her team volunteered themselves as test cases. By August of 1972, Tu was able to perform clinical trials of artemisinin on thirty malaria patients. Tu presented the drug at a World Health Organization meeting on malaria in 1981 and the Chinese Ministry of Health finally officially approved artemisinin in 1986, fifteen years after Project 523 began.

In the 1990s, artemisinin gradually began replacing previous generations of medicines that had lost their effectiveness. Artemisinin was effective against even the most stubborn strains of malaria. In severe cases where patients were hospitalized, artemisinin cut the mortality rate in half. World Health Organization statistics for 2013 showed that malaria deaths had fallen from about two million per year a decade earlier to an estimated 584,000.

There was some controversy attached to Tu's 2015 Nobel Prize in Physiology or Medicine, as hundreds of scientists had been involved. However, it was Tu herself who brought in the sweet wormwood plant and created a method for extracting the active ingredient, as well as leading the first human trials.

Frances Oldham Kelsey

A medical crisis need not be germ-based to spread dangerously. Beginning in 1960, tens of thousands of babies were born with improperly developed limbs, and, in some cases, malfunctioning eyes, ears, or other organs. It was a tragedy as had never been seen before, catastrophically striking families in more than forty countries, including Germany, Japan, and England. The cause of these birth defects was a new sedative called thalidomide, which had been approved to treat pregnant women for morning sickness. It seemed like a godsend, especially for women with hyperemesis gravidarum, which is like morning sickness gone nuclear, and can become a serious health problem. The studies done on this drug were limited in scope and did not reveal its devastating side effects. It was quickly taken off the market, but for the many babies who were hurt or killed, the damage was done.

So why were thalidomide birth defects rampant in Europe but rare in America? It was largely because of one woman, new drug reviewer Frances Oldham Kelsey. Born in 1914 in British Columbia, Kelsey earned both a bachelor and master of science from McGill University. In the mid-1930s, Kelsey wrote to Eugene Geiling, a researcher at the University of Chicago, asking to work in his lab and study for a doctorate. Dr. Geiling replied with an offer of a scholarship for "Mr. Oldham." Thankfully, he still honored his offer when Ms. Oldham arrived.

In 1938, Oldham earned her PhD from the University of Chicago and would later join the faculty there. She married Dr. Fremont Ellis Kelsey, a fellow professor, in 1943 and the couple had two daughters, all while Frances Kelsey earned her medical degree. Kelsey moved to Washington, DC, to begin her long, distinguished career with the Food and Drug Administration, where she became chief of the Division of New Drugs, director of the Division of Scientific Investigations, and deputy for Scientific and Medical Affairs Office of Compliance.

Kelsey was assigned to review applications from pharmaceutical companies for drug approval. It was a job she was well-suited to, have already proven herself to be masterful detective. While earning her PhD in pharmacology, Kelsey helped pinpoint a toxic ingredient in another drug called elixir sulfanilamide. Elixir sulfanilamide was marketed as something of a cure-all, which should always raise an eyebrow. The drug was very bitter, so the manufacturer added a sweetener. That sweetener, Kelsey discovered, was antifreeze. The drug had already killed more than a hundred people by the time the FDA got it off the market.

Do not drink this.

While it's imperative to keep antifreeze away from children and pets, it's a wives' tale that cats will drink it because of its sweet taste. Cats can't taste sweet at all.

When the paperwork for thalidomide, sold under the brand name Kevadon, hit Kelsey's desk in the fall of 1960, she was expected to approve it automatically, since it was already popular in Europe. Her critical eye, however, quickly spotted holes in the data "proving" that thalidomide was safe, and she rejected the application. The "results" in their application were more testimonials than quantifiable science, and the developers had failed to do a placental barrier test to show whether the drug would reach the fetus when taken by a pregnant woman. A chemist working under Kelsey who spoke German also pointed out a higher-than-acceptable number of translation errors in the English copy of the application. In something of a baptism by fire, the thalidomide application was the first Kelsey handled in her new position. There was significant push-back as the drug company lodged complaints against Kelsey with her superiors. Nevertheless, for the next fourteen months, she did not budge. In November 1961, Dr. Kelsey's careful vigilance was vindicated when Kevadon was taken off the market in its native West Germany and in other countries soon after.

In the aftermath of thalidomide's European release, thousands of children in Europe were born with partial limbs, blindness, deafness, and/or cognitive impairment. Those who did not die in utero, that is, which is thought to be four times as many. Thalidomide's effects on fetal development are so dramatic and predictable that doctors can pinpoint in which week of pregnancy the mother took it by which fetal body system was affected. Kelsey's steadfastness prevented the same from happening in the US. Sadly, this does not mean there were no "children of thalidomide" in the States. Drug reps had given out samples without FDA approval, but the US had only about 1 percent the number of cases seen abroad.

CHAPTER 2

Culture & Religion

SURPRISE POLYGLOT

English is the third most widely used language in the world, behind Mandarin and Spanish, with about one in seven people worldwide able to speak it. There are about 375 million native speakers and about 220 million more people use it as their second language. It's often used for work and travel, making it the most international language today.

English 101

English began as a Germanic language, not a Romance language, as many people assume. Romance languages, like French, Italian, Spanish, and Romanian, come from the far western reaches of the Roman Empire, where people spoke common, or vulgar, Latin. Germanic tribes (Saxons, Angles, from whom we get the word "English," and Jutes) came to Britain around 449 CE, pushing out the Celtic Britons or making them speak English instead of the old Celtic languages. Some Celtic languages, like Welsh, Irish Gaelic, and Scottish Gallic, are still hanging on today. The Germanic dialects of these different tribes became what is now called Old English. Old English did not sound or look much like the English spoken today. If a time machine dropped you off back then, and you did not immediately kill everyone around you with disease, you would be unlikely to understand more than a few words. Around 800 CE, Danish and Norse pirates, also called Vikings, came to the country and established Danelaw, adding many Norse loanwords.

Not all Nordic people were Vikings, not even the Vikings. The word *viking* is a verb, to leave one's home for adventure and fortune, and those who did it were *vikingrs*. The majority of people were farmers and tradespeople, just like in other countries.

And they didn't wear helmets with horns like this one. Sorry, everybody.

When William the Conqueror took over England in 1066 CE, he brought his nobles, who spoke Norman, a language closely related to French. Because all official documents were written in Norman, English changed a great deal at that point, taking in words and dropping word endings. This was Middle English, the era of Geoffrey Chaucer and his *Canterbury Tales*. If a time machine dropped you off and the people did not immediately kill *you* with disease, you would be able to pick out a few more words you recognize.

If you are wondering where Shakespearean English falls in the timeline, that's considered Early Modern English. Apart from words we do not use anyone and words that have completely changed their meaning, Early Modern English sounded distinctly different from Modern English (the language, not the band) because of the "great vowel shift." This was the gradual change in the pronunciation of long vowels, moving them from the front of the mouth to the back over the course of a century or so. "House" was originally pronounced "hoos," "one" used to be "own," "plead" was "pled" and so forth. So, if your time machine let you out here, you would probably get by about as well as you did reading Shakespeare in high school.

Scientists and scholars from different countries and cultures needed to talk to one another, so they named things in the languages they all knew: Greek and Latin. Some of those words were absorbed into everyday English, like photograph ("photo" meaning light and "graph" meaning "picture" or "writing" in Greek).

Brother, Can You Spare a Lexicon?

Many other people came to England later at different times, as happens when you colonize half the world. They brought with them different languages, and these languages added more words to make today's English. English continues to take in new words from other languages, mainly from French (around 30 to 40 percent of our vocabulary), but from many other languages as well. So, a native English speaker is in fact speaking Old English, Danish, Norse, French, Latin, Greek, Chinese, Hindi, Japanese, Dutch, Spanish, and other languages, and they do not even know it.

Our language sucks up foreign words like a vacuum. For example, English took over 1,700 loanwords from French. Loanwords are words adopted from one language and incorporated into another without translation; they simply become part of that vocabulary as-is. English has given words to other languages too, especially in the modern technological era, with things like "email," "computer," and "mobile." That's not a new phenomenon, and it's not just tech. After Friday, the French enjoy *le weekend*. In an ironic twist, the word "loanword" itself is borrowed from German, but it's not a loanword. It's a "calque," or loan translation: a word or phrase that borrows its meaning from another language by translating into existing words in the target language. For example, "commonplace" is a calque of Latin *locus commūnis*.

The examples of words in English borrowed from French, German, Spanish, and Italian are ridiculously numerous. This is hardly surprising due to the close geographic ties that the countries and, therefore the languages, traditionally share. These cousin countries are by no means the only languages that have contributed words. *Ombudsman*, *ski*, and *smorgasbord* arrived from Scandinavia. *Icon* and *vodka* arrived from Russia. *Avatar*, *karma*, and *yoga* are Sanskrit words.

German

German has given us words of many types, but food words are by far the largest category: *knackwurst*, *liverwurst*, *noodle*, *pumpernickel*, *sauerkraut*, *pretzel*, and *lager*. There are also science-y words, like *feldspar*, *quartz*, and *hex*. It has even lent us the names of some dogs, not only the obvious *dachshund*, but also *poodle*, which I would have laid money was French. A great deal more German words came over during the last century, on account of those pesky world wars. That's when we got *blitzkrieg*, *zeppelin*, *strafe*, and *U-boat*, but also another round of food words, like *delicatessen*, *hamburger*, *frankfurter* and *wiener*, *bundt* as in the cake, *spritz* as in cookie, and *strudel*. And let's not forget about *kindergarten* for the children and *Oktoberfest* (which is actually September) for the adults.

Thanks, Germany!

German used to be the second most common language in the US. It was so prevalent that entire city governments operated in and school systems taught exclusively in German. That was prior to WWI. When the war started, official use of German was phased out in a hurry.

Dutch

We have the Dutch to thank for many familiar nautical terms. *Avast, boom, buoy, commodore, cruise, dock, keel, reef, skipper, smuggle, tackle,* and *yacht* are all Dutch words, as are *freight, scoop, leak, scour, splice,* and *pump.* If you work with fabric, you have certainly had your *spool* run out at a bad time. The mother tongue of Van Gogh also gave us *easel, etching, landscape,* and *sketch.* War pops up yet again in the form of *holster, furlough, onslaught,* and others. Let's go back to food, where Dutch gave English the words *booze, brandy, coleslaw, cookie, cranberry, crullers, gin, hops,* and, of course, *waffle.* (An aside, not only are terms like "Dutch treat" and "Dutch courage" not loan phrases, they are old-timey, sarcastic insults, so let's try to stop using them.)

Hindi

How much Hindi do you know? A lot more than you think. You wake up in your *bungalow* with its *chintz* curtains, change out of your *pajamas,* and into your *dungarees* and fetching *bandana,* because you are all about that *thug* life, until you realize you forgot to *shampoo* your hair and no one put away *punch* from the party last night. But you are fierce, you are a *juggernaut.* You hop on your train to the city for your day in the concrete *jungle.*

African Languages

Speaking to African languages as a broad group, which they are, English has taken the words *banana, banjo, boogie-woogie, chigger* (nasty, little tick-like things), *goober* (a.k.a. peanuts), *gorilla, gumbo, jazz, jitterbug, jitters, juke* (as in -box), *voodoo, yam, zebra,* and *zombie.*

Native American Languages

Lumping another vast and diverse group of people's languages into one paragraph are the loanwords from North American natives. There are hundreds or even thousands of place names that use the words of the people that were driven out of them: Ottawa, Toronto, Saskatchewan (which boasts a town called Moosejaw), and the names of more than half the states of the US, including Michigan, Texas, Nebraska, and Illinois, even though it looks French. (The city of Detroit *is* French; it means "the narrows.") Native American languages also gave us the food words *avocado, chocolate, squash, pecan, potato, tomato, chili,* and *cannibal.* There are animal names like *chipmunk, woodchuck, possum, moose,* and *skunk.* Plus *canoe, toboggan, moccasin, hammock, hurricane, tobacco, tomahawk,* and the turtles known as *terrapins.*

And now I'm hungry.

A brief detour for the word, *squaw.* You may have cringed when you read it. " 'Oh no,' you say to yourself, '*Squaw* is a slur, like calling a Roma person a G*psy.' " That's not wholly true, though. First and foremost, regardless of what a word is, where it came from, or what it meant originally, if that word is being used as an insult, then it is an insult. There *are* those who use the word *squaw* to demean Native women. That aside, people believe that *squaw* is inherently insulting because they have been told it comes from the Mohawk *ojiskwa*, a vulgar word for female genitalia. This etymology is highly unlikely, since in the Algonquin language family, *squaw* simply means "woman" or "young woman." It was in no way pejorative and was even used in missionary translations of the Bible. It can be seen in that context in writings dating back to the 1600s. There is a movement in some Native American communities to reclaim the word and remove the stigma. As one Abenaki woman writes, "When our languages are perceived as dirty words, we and our grandchildren are in grave danger of losing our self-respect."

Oy Vey!

Arguably, the best language to season the stew of English is Yiddish. Let's start the explanation of what Yiddish is by telling you what it is not. Yiddish is not Hebrew. Though they are both historically used by Jews, share an alphabet that contains no capital letters, and are read from right to left, they are not the same language. One reason the two get mixed up in people's minds is that Yiddish speakers usually learn to read Hebrew in childhood, since holy texts and prayers are written in classical Hebrew. However, this form of Hebrew is markedly different from the modern Hebrew spoken in Israel. You can think of Yiddish as the international language of the Ashkenazi Jews of Eastern Europe, who typically spoke it in addition to the dominant language in their area. Yiddish is referred to as *mame loshn*, or "mother tongue." The word "Yiddish" is the Yiddish word for Jewish, so while it is technically correct to refer to speaking Yiddish as "speaking Jewish," it is inadvisable to do so. At its height less than a century ago, Yiddish was understood by an estimated eleven million of the world's eighteen million Jews. Now, due largely to WWII, three times more people speak Hebrew than Yiddish. Fewer than a quarter-million people in the United States speak Yiddish, about half of them are living in Texas. Just kidding, they are in New York. Where else was it going to be? In recent years, Yiddish has experienced a resurgence and is now being taught at universities, and there are Yiddish Studies departments at Columbia and Oxford.

Now, let's get to the Yiddish you are speaking without even knowing it. To quote Bill Murray in the holiday classic *Scrooged*, "The Jews have a great word—*schmuck*. I was a *schmuck*. Now, I'm not a *schmuck*." *Schmuck* is a word for the male member, as are *putz*, *schvantz*, and *schlong*. You use one of those to *schtup*. If you think I am being too bold, you might give me a slap on the *tuchis*. What can I say? I've got a lot of *chutzpah*. And it kills me to hear people say "chootspah." *Oy vey*. When you see the *ch*, give it a *hhhh* sound. We should go out for a drink and a *nosh*, maybe a *bagel* and a *schmear*. Can you pay? I've got no money, *bupkes*. And can we drive? The coffee shop is a bit of a *schlep*. Nice place, I had a meeting there when I was trying to *schmooze* a new client. I go through my whole *spiel* and I am super nervous, feeling like a *yutz*. Finally, he says "Yeah, I like your *shtick*." I don't think I could work at a coffee shop, though. I'd be spilling drinks all over people, I am such a *klutz*. Plus, you hear these coffee *mavens* talk about this one's Indonesian, this one's Sumatra; they all taste like burned bean water to me. C'mere, you got a little *schmutz* on your face. There you go.

There are more, of course. *Zaftig* means having a pleasingly plump figure. *Glitch* is also Yiddish, though it originally meant a slip-up. Before we leave the Yiddishkeit, let's look at the intro to the classic TV show *Laverne & Shirley*, "Schlemiel! Schlimazel! Hasenpfeffer Incorporated!" A *schlemiel* is a fool. *Schlimazel* means a quarrel or a fight. *Hasenpfeffer* is not Yiddish; it's a type of German stew, usually made with rabbit.

Fantabulosa

Another fascinating language added to our lexicon isn't technically a language. Polari is a cant, a cryptolect, also sometimes called an anti-language, a system of slang based on the speaker's native language, used only by a select group. For gay men in Britain before 1967, Polari was not just cute jargon; it was absolutely necessary. Being gay or even being perceived as gay could land you in prison for "gross indecency." It was taboo to write or speak the words "gay" or "homosexual." Gay people needed a way to talk about their relationships and the other aspects of their lives without being understood by eavesdroppers. Polari came about as a form of insider slang, built from different languages, shifting and changing as it evolved. Language professor Paul Baker summed Polari up in his 2002 book *Polari—The Lost Language of Gay Men*, it was a lingo of "fast put-downs, ironic self-parody, and theatrical exaggeration."

Cockney rhyming slang replaces words with entire phrases, then shortens them. The word for telephone is *dog*. The first step was to rhyme something with "telephone," which was the phrase "dog and bone." That's a bit wordy, so two-thirds of it was dropped. Likewise, "feet" became *plates*, through "plates of meat," and "stairs" became *apples* through "apples and pears."

Although Polari saw the height of its popularity in the mid-twentieth century, its roots are much older. A similar argot called Parlyaree had been spoken in markets and fairgrounds at least as early as the eighteenth century, made up partly of Romany words with selections from thieves' cant and backslang—words that are spelled and spoken phonemically backward, such as *yob* for boy and *riah* for hair. It also included, by way of the theater, the "broken Italian" used by street puppeteers who put on Punch and Judy shows. Even the name Polari is an Anglicization of an Italian word, *parlare*, "to speak." As its use spread, it picked up bits of French, Yiddish, Italian, Shelta (the language of the Irish Travelers), London slang, and Cockney rhyming slang, among others.

Besides being useful for discussing intimate business, Polari could be used to determine if someone else was gay. You could drop a few words into a conversation to see if the other person picked up on it. If they did not, no harm done. As such, the Polari glossary evolved to include a number of racy terms, so that people could set up rendezvous or discuss recent conquests without blowing their cover. *Trade* is a gay sex partner. *TBH* stands for "to be had," which described that a person was sexually available, what we call today "DTF." In Polari, an *omi* is a man, and a woman is a *dona* or a *palone*. An *omi-palone* is an effeminate man, or sometimes just a gay one. If you flip it around, a *palone-omi* is a lesbian. The best-known Polarism is *drag*, referring to women's clothing when worn by men, possibly stemming from a Romany words for skirt. Where there is drag, someone is going to *zhoosh* something up. An effeminate gay man is a bit *camp*, and he may *mince* as he walks. A masculine man, or masculine anything for that matter, is *butch*. Does he have a nice *bod*? That's Polari, too.

GOOD MOURNING TO YOU

When I die, there won't be a funeral. That's not to say my body would not be properly taken care of. Obviously it will be, or my cats will eat me.

They'd probably wait at least an hour.

What I am staunchly against are those depressing affairs full of silent discomfort and, worst thing of all, the viewing. Thankfully, there is a literal world of funeral practice options to choose from, everything from an Irish wake to Tibetan sky burial. Talking about death need not be depressing. Death is a part of life, and we should be able to talk about death as easily as we talk about birth. They are fundamentally the same—a momentous life event that your family deals with more than you do and tends to be at least a little messy.

The Second Line

There are as many ways to celebrate a person's life as there are kinds of people in the world. So, in the spirit of celebration, we begin close to home with the New Orleans jazz funeral. Along with Mardi Gras beads and a bowl of gumbo, the boisterous, jazz-fueled funeral procession is one of the prototypical images of New Orleans, Louisiana. In olden times, European-Americans attended funerals with brass bands playing solemn music on the way to the grave and happy music on the return. With the end of slavery, black funerals with brass bands became more common, incorporating the new music style of jazz as it developed. At the same time, brass bands for funerals fell out of favor with white New Orleanians. Fusing West African, French, and African American traditions, these funeral processions strike a unique balance between joy and grief as mourners are led by a marching band. The band plays sorrowful dirges at first, but, once the body is buried, the volume and the tempo go up. The "main line" or "first line" is the main section of the parade, those who actually have the permit for the parade, as well as the band. Those who follow the band, dancing as they go, are called the "second line."

Hinduism

In Hinduism, death is not viewed as the end of life but as a change in the journey of your *atman*, or soul. The traditional mourning period is limited to thirteen days. It's thought that if someone laments too much, it will harm the soul of the deceased. Immediately after the person dies, an oil lamp is placed near the body, which stays burning for three days, though the body should be cremated the day after death. From then until the thirteenth day, the decedent's immediate family is considered to be ritually impure. They might bathe twice daily, wear white, eat only one vegetarian meal each day, and refrain from religious rites and festivals. When they reach the thirteenth day, a *shaddra* is performed. This ceremony involves a fire sacrifice. Offerings are given to both the gods and their ancestors, to ensure a peaceful afterlife. The family washes the family shrine, leaving more offerings for the gods, and the mourning period is complete.

Buddhism

Buddhists, like Hindus, believe in reincarnation. Buddhist traditions involve a funeral with three components: sharing, conducting yourself well, and meditating. Similar to Christian funerals, the ceremony takes place at a funeral home and includes a eulogy and prayers. Funerals differ from country to country, but usually include an open casket. This is because when someone looks at the body, it serves as a reminder of the impermanence of life, a communal *momento muri*.

Islam

Islam also requires a specific period of mourning, though theirs is three days. During that time, the family should avoid wearing jewelry or decorative clothing. Widows should mourn for four lunar months plus ten days, during which time they also should not remarry or move to a new home. It's acceptable to show your grief by crying but wailing or tearing at hair and clothes is frowned upon. Islamic custom also calls for burial to be soon after death, in some places as quickly as the same day. In Iran specifically, the body is prepared for burial by being washed nine times and wrapped in a white shroud. It's considered quite a holy act to help carry the coffin, so funeral processions often involve huge crowds around the coffin itself. During the burial, the body is placed in a grave facing Mecca, the most holy location on Earth for Muslims, and is surrounded by weeping mourners reciting prayers from the *Qur'an*. The mourning afterwards is divided into significant days. On the third day, a memorial service is held with huge flower arrangements and rosewater sprinkled everywhere. On the seventh day, the grave is visited, and food is given to the poor. On the fortieth day, the mourners, who have been wearing black, may begin wearing their normal clothes again, and a gravestone is put on the grave.

What to Wear

On the subject of wearing black, while it may be the color of mourning for many cultures and countries, it's not universal. Catholics in Brazil may wear purple, as do people in Thailand. White is the favored color in much of East Asia and for Australian aborigines, as it symbolizes purity and rebirth. It was also the custom for a time in Europe, specifically for children and unmarried women. Red is the modern color for mourning in South Africa, symbolizing the bloodshed of apartheid.

The Tower of Silence

Among the world's oldest religions is Zoroastrianism, a monotheistic faith that has been continuously practiced for 3,500 years. Their funeral practices involved a place with the Games of Thrones-sounding name, the Tower of Silence. The Tower of Silence is a large, round stone building with no roof. After death, a body could be contaminated by demons, but it can be protected and made pure by exposing it to the elements—the sun, the wind, and carrion birds. Bodies are arranged on the towers in concentric circles, with men placed in the outer circle, women in the middle, and children in the inner circle. Bodies are left until they are reduced to white bones, which are then placed in ossuaries near or inside the towers.

> The legendary frontman of Queen, Freddie Mercury, was Zoroastrian. His funeral was conducted by a Zoroastrian priest and his body was cremated. In accordance with his wishes, his best friend, Mary Austin, has kept his ashes hidden, and she swears she will never reveal their location.

You would not think our ailing environment could have an impact on funerals, but for Zoroastrians, it really does. Habitat destruction was already doing enough damage to the vulture population before a livestock drug was developed in the early 1990s that proved toxic to the vultures feeding on cow carcasses. The drug was banned in May 2006, but by then it had decimated 95 percent of the vulture population in the region.

Sky Burial

Vultures also play a key role in the sky burial traditions of Tibet and Mongolia. In those cold, rocky mountains, burying bodies in the ground is difficult. When a person dies, their body is wrapped in white cloth and monks or lamas read scriptures aloud so that the soul can be released from purgatory. The home is kept peaceful to ease the soul's ascension to the heavens. When the prayer period is over, the body is be taken to the sky burial site high in the mountains to await bearded vultures. A special burial master sections the body and lays it out for the vultures, who they call *dakinis* or "sky dancers." The vultures eat the body and take it up into the heavens. If that's a little hard for you to digest, no pun intended, remember that a body buried in the ground gets eaten, too, just by things that are much, much smaller.

They're Just Sleeping

In Tana Toraja in eastern Indonesia, funerals are raucous affairs involving the whole village and can last from days to weeks. Families save up far in advance to pay for a lavish funeral, where sacrificial water buffalo will carry the deceased's soul to the afterlife. They have time to save the money because the funeral does not happen until years after death. In the meantime, the dead relative is referred to simply as a "person who is sick" or even one "who is asleep." They are laid down special rooms in the family home, where they are symbolically fed, cared for, and remain an important part of their relatives' lives.

Turning the Bones

The dead remain in the lives of the Malagasy people of Madagascar through their practice of *famadihana* or the turning of the bones. Once every five or seven years, the family has a celebration at its ancestral crypt where the bodies are exhumed, wrapped in new silk shrouds, and sprayed with wine or perfume. It's a lively event where a band plays while family members dance with the bodies. The Malagasy believe their ancestors serve as intermediaries between the living and God, with the power to intervene in events on Earth until their body has completely decomposed. Once the revelry subsides, the bodies are replaced in their tombs with gifts of money and alcohol. This is done before sunset because the sun is the source of energy.

Australian Aborigines

Tending to a dead loved one in the Aboriginal society in Australia's Northern Territory begins with a smoking ceremony held where the deceased lived to drive away their spirit. Next, a feast is prepared. Mourners are painted with ochre, a natural, yellow pigment, as they eat and dance. The body is traditionally placed atop a platform like a funeral pyre, except the body is covered with leaves and allowed to decompose. In some traditions, if the person was the victim of murder, fluids draining from the platform are believed to help identify the killer.

An Ounce of Flesh

Some cultures believe a physical representation of emotional pain is essential to the grieving process. Some members of the Dani tribe of Papua-New Guinea tribe will cut off the tip of a finger. This ritual is specific to women, who will cut off a section of a finger if they lose a family member, especially a child. The practice is done to both placate the spirits and to provide a way to use physical pain as an expression of sorrow and suffering. They numb the finger by tying a string tightly around it ahead of time, which also controls the bleeding. The section of finger is then dried and either cremated or stored in a special place. This may seem extreme to us, but it's an important part of their cultural identity and every bit as valid as putting makeup on the dead so they look "natural" or leaving them flowers they cannot smell.

No Funeral for You!

In many of the diverse peoples of Africa, it's believed that witches and sorcerers are not admitted to the spirit world and are consequently denied a proper burial. The same applies to anyone who was generally a bad person. Those not buried rightfully are refused admittance to the afterlife and become wandering spirits. They roam the physical realm aimlessly and wreak havoc whenever they can. They are cut off from the community of their ancestors, the nearest equivalent to Hell in those cultures. As with the Malagasy, these communities believe an ancestor can intercede for the living and to be in the community of ancestors is a continuation of life. What constitutes a "proper burial" varies from culture to culture, of course. The Abaluya of Kenya bury their dead naked as a preparatory stage for rebirth in the next world.

The Seat of Power

To the Asante of Ghana, the stool is a highly important object, representing power and unity and denotes the office of a high chieftain. When a new chief is enthroned, he is given his own special stool, which he must never abandon. When a chief dies, the stool becomes the abode of their spirit. It's ceremonially blackened, first by smoking it, then smearing it with kitchen soot and egg yolk. From then, the black stool becomes an ancestral seat, a permanent reminder of the beloved ruler. It's guarded in a special room, where it's placed on animal skins or rugs so that it does not touch the ground. Sacrifices are made to the stool and it's brought out for festivals. Before a new chief may take his throne, he must bare his chest and kneel before the black stool of his predecessor in humility and respect. Elsewhere in Ghana, some people aspire to be buried in fantasy coffins that represent their work or something they loved in life. You might see a coffin shaped like a Mercedes-Benz for a businessman, a giant fish coffin for a fisherman, or a coffin in the shape of a Bible for someone particularly devout. In America, we have more options in coffins and caskets, including biodegradable alternatives for green burials, made of materials like willow, bamboo, or sea grass, but they tend to be rectangular in shape.

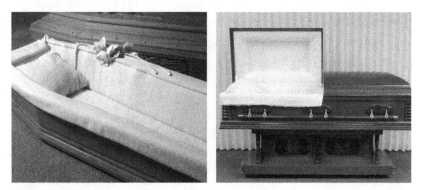

A coffin versus a casket.

The primary difference between a coffin and a casket is the shape. Coffins are wider at the shoulder and narrow at the feet, like you see in old horror movies and Halloween decorations. Caskets are plain rectangles.

Accessories

The Banyankole tribe of Uganda holds a special death ritual for people who die while harboring a grudge. They bury the corpses of the grudge-holder with various objects to occupy the grumpy spirit, so they won't have the time or inclination to haunt people. When a married person in the Buganda tribe dies, the corpse is buried wearing the underwear of the surviving spouse. If the deceased is a man, his wife dresses him up in her underwear, while saying aloud to him that he has gone to the grave with his wife. This death ritual deceives the ghost of the dead spouse, convincing them that they have been buried with their spouse, so they won't haunt the living spouse by seeking marital relations with them.

The Party Never Stops

Some clans of the Igbo of Nigeria still practice a ritual of burying their chief or the head of a family in an upright position with a long funnel leading from above the ground right into his open mouth. The family will then feed the departed with palm wine or other spirits. In addition to making sure the deceased does not miss the party, it helps to maintain the bonds between the dead and the living, ensuring the deceased's name is never forgotten.

Ashes to Ashes

In South Africa, the windows of a house in which a death has occurred may be smeared with ash, all the beds are removed from the dead person's room so mourners can enter, and sometimes a ritual sacrifice of an animal may be done to please ancestors. After the funeral, everyone must wash off the dust and dirt from the graveyard before they enter the house, to wash off bad luck.

An Ox Coffin for Diamond Dogs

Statistically speaking a number of people reading this are fans of the late great David Bowie, but you may not know that his wish for his mortal remains was *Ngaben*, the traditional Balinese cremation ceremony. Like an Irish wake or a New Orleans second line, the *Ngaben* is a long celebration of life. Most Balinese practice a form of Hinduism unique to the island, which mixes

Hindu beliefs with Buddhism and local traditional animist practices. The ritual's name comes from the word *ngabuin* or *ngabu*, which means "turn to ash." The family will construct a *wadah*, a tower-like structure built of papier-mache, wood, and bamboo, and a *lembu*, a sarcophagus in the shape of an ox. Royals and high-caste people have *lembu* in the shape of other animals, such as a lion or dragon. The deceased is placed in the *wadah* and is taken to the cremation site in a joyful, parade-like procession. The body is transferred to the *lembu* and a priest oversees the burning of the body. Twelve days after the cremation, the ashes are scattered into the sea or a river leading to the sea in a final act of purification.

Conversely

One culture has mourning traditions that are definitely an inverse of most—they mourn birth. The nomadic Bopa and Kalbeliya tribes of Rajistan accompany the bodies of their dead to the cremation pyre with dancing and great revelry, celebrating the soul being freed from the prison of its body. Conversely, they mourn when a new baby is born, as continued reincarnation is viewed as divine punishment.

BAPTISM BY...

There are lots of religions out there with multiple sacraments apiece, so we are going to define baptism in broad terms as an act or experience that makes a person an official part of a community. In the Christian church, baptism involves water as a symbol of purification and is typically accompanied by giving the initiate their name, particularly in the case of babies, who are the most likely to be baptized. In addition to Baptists, there are Anabaptists, a Christian movement that traces its origins to the Radical Reformation (Martin Luther's little kerfuffle). Anabaptists believe that baptism is valid only when the candidate *wants* to be baptized, so they are baptized as adults. Of the four million or so Anabaptists throughout the world, the most numerous include the Mennonites, the German Baptists, and the Amish.

Buddhism

As in Christianity, many infant baptism practices include officially naming the child. When a baby is born into a Buddhist family in parts of Asia, monks are invited to the house to bless the baby and chant from the holy texts. Based on the exact time and date of the birth, an astrologer will draw a horoscope and advise the parents about the initial that the baby's name should begin with. Within one month of birth, the baby is brought to a temple for blessing and placed before a statue of the Buddha. Offerings of flowers, candles, and incense are made, and the monk blesses the child, announcing his or her name. In some forms of Buddhism, sacred threads are tied around the baby's wrists to welcome *Khwan*, a spirit that looks after babies.

All Chinese children of a generation share the same middle name and there is a cycle of twenty-four generation names, which can take several hundred years to get through.

Arctic Natives

The Native people of the Arctic lands in north Canada, Alaska, and Greenland hold a naming ceremony called *atiq*, which means both "name" and "spirit." The baby is given the name of a family member who has died, usually a beloved older relative. They chose the relative if the baby has a similar birthmark to that person or if the mother dreamed about them during pregnancy. The Inuit believe in reincarnation and that the child receives the relative's spirit along with the name. It's also believed that a baby who cries incessantly when born will stop crying once the right *atiq* is given.

Islam

There is a tradition in some Muslim cultures called *Aqiqah*. As soon as a Muslim baby is born, the father or grandfather whispers a prayer in their ear so that it is the first thing they hear. Names are usually chosen from the *Qur'an*, and the *Aqiqah* is held within seven days of birth. Prayers are said and the baby's head is shaved. The hair is weighed, and the family gives at least the same weight in gold or silver to charity. The baby is then given a taste of honey as a symbol of the sweetness of prayer. (Though this tradition probably goes back more than two thousand years, babies less than one year old should not eat honey, as it may contain botulism spores that their little bodies can't fight off.) *Aqiqah* also includes a feast for friends and relatives with one-third of the meat distributed to the poor.

Honey: tasty, sweet, but not great for babies.

Sikh

Soon after the birth of a Sikh baby, a respected elder gives them a few drops of honeyed water while reciting a hymn. Once the mother and baby are well enough, a naming ceremony is held at the *gurudwara*, the Sikh temple. There is a reading from the Sikh holy book, *Siri Guru Granth Sahib*, where the passage is selected at random. The first letter of the word at the beginning of this passage will be the first letter of the baby's name, which is then chosen by the parents. All boys are given the same second name, Singh, meaning "lion," and for all girls, Kaur, meaning "princess." Family and friends are given *kara prashad*, a sweet treat made with flour, sugar and clarified butter, followed by a communal meal.

Tanzania

Among the Akamba people of Tanzania, a child is named on the third day following their birth. Before the naming ceremony, the newborn is regarded as a spirit and not as a complete human being. A goat is slaughtered in appreciation of the ancestral spirits for the gift of a child and the fertility of the parents. The climax of the ceremony is the announcement of the baby's name by their grandmother or an elder female relative.

Life and Death

While baptisms are usually joyous celebrations of life, tragedy can show up uninvited. In 2013, a Seattle area baptism turned into a drunken brawl and law enforcement had to be called in. The incident ended with five police officers assaulted, two officers injured, and two people in jail. In 2014, a Florida man was fatally shot at a baptism party when he tried to break up a fight over food between the family and some party-crashers. That same year, an adult baptism was held on the beach in California, when seven foot (or two meter) waves swept three people away. Two were able to swim back to shore, but one was never found. A similar tragedy occurred in 2018 in South Africa, where rip currents drowned three men. In 2005, Reverend Kyle Lake was electrocuted when he reached out to adjust a microphone while standing in the baptismal water. Fortunately, the woman who was being baptized had not yet gotten into the water, so she was not injured. The reverend's widow later received a settlement from the electrical contractor on the basis that the company had negligently designed, assembled, and installed heaters in the font that resulted in the electrocution.

A Florida Man

Baptism isn't immune to weirdness, either. In 2016, a Florida man claimed that the voice of God woke him in the middle of the night and commanded him to baptize his son. So, the man woke up his eleven-year-old son and dunked him repeatedly in a neighbor's pool, which was green and full of leaves and bugs. The boy got an ear and eye infection from the water, and the father was charged with child abuse.

We hear so many wacky "Florida man" stories because arrest records in Florida are public, making them more likely to wind up on the news.

Just the Tip

Another common ritual to show that a child is now part of their parents' religion or community is circumcision. The mind goes immediately to Jewish baby boys, who have their foreskins removed eight days after birth in a ceremony called a *bris*, but "the chosen people" are hardly the only people who practice circumcision. Rates of male circumcision vary, from virtually 0 percent in Honduras, to 7 percent in Spain, 20 percent in the United Kingdom, 45 percent in South Africa, 80 percent in the United States, to over 90 percent in many Muslim-majority countries. Traditional circumcision isn't limited to one infant and one officiant. Take the practice of *imbalu* of the Bambasaba and Bakusu people of Uganda. Held during the rainy season every other year, *imbalu* is a ceremony of mass circumcision, where hundreds of young men, from sixteen to their mid-twenties, are initiated through circumcision. The candidates are expected to stand firm as a sign of courage and boldness. The young men dress in traditional garments made of plantain fronds and animal hides and declare their intentions to be circumcised. Elders lead them to be circumcised while dancing and singing, accompanied by friends, cheering and dancing through the streets. Crying during the process would mean cowardice and is forbidden. The actual circumcision segment lasts about one hour, as the surgeon goes through the young men, making three cuts to remove each foreskin. A whistle is blown when the last circumcision is done. The young men are led to a quiet place and wrapped in a cloth until the bleeding stops. They then go their fathers' homes and are hand-fed for three days before being ritually washed and permitted to eat with their hands, marking the end of the ritual. While most circumcision is carried out in private with a few people present, the i*mbalu* is a public function and has actually become a tourist attraction.

Tradition Versus Contagion

Back to Jewish infant circumcision and a rare ancient ritual called *metzitzeh b'peh*, which requires that the blood from the incision be removed by the *mohel*, the rabbi performing the *bris*, by mouth. Normally, nothing much comes of it, unless your *mohel* has herpes. Since 2006, 22 percent of male neonatal herpes cases in New York City were linked to ritual circumcision. Herpes is a nuisance infection to adults, but can be dangerous in newborns, quickly spreading throughout the body. Of the twenty-two cases of *mohel*-spread herpes since 2000, two babies suffered permanent brain damage, and two died. The city Board of Health has tried requiring written consent and distributing pamphlets warning that "some babies can get herpes, which can even lead to death" following *metzitzah b'peh*. Health officials worry that parents are not seeing the brochures, due in no small part to the insular nature of some ultra-Orthodox communities. Leaders of the communities that practice *metzitzeh b'peh* have opposed any restrictions on the centuries-old ritual as an infringement on their religious freedom.

Baptized in the Afterlife

Some groups baptize babies, some baptize adults, and some baptize the dead. It does not even have to be their own dead. The Mormons, or to give them their full name, the Church of Jesus Christ of Latter-Day Saints, have practiced baptism of the dead since 1840. Posthumous or proxy baptisms are performed at the church's 159 temples, where members the same gender as the dead person, usually young people, are immersed in an ornate baptismal font which rests on statutes of twelve oxen. The baptism is then recorded in a database. The LDS Church has built the world's most extensive genealogical library in Salt Lake City with seven hundred employees and more than two billion names. Mormons believe that vicarious baptisms give the deceased, who exist in the afterlife as conscious spirits, a final chance to join the Mormon fold, and thus, gain access to the Celestial Kingdom. It's only *supposed* to be performed for one's own family. The LDS Church is the only major religion that currently baptizes the dead, and that has contributed to some bad press in the past few decades, particularly when they baptized Jewish Holocaust victims and celebrities, like "Crocodile Hunter" Steve Irwin. LDS leaders emphasize that the spirits of the dead must accept the baptism and have reminded church members to only baptize family members, particularly after Jewish genealogists discovered in the 1990s that 380,000 Holocaust survivors had been vicariously baptized. One reason Holocaust victims are such a common target is that their names are easy to find in government records, which creates an efficient way to quickly baptize more people. The baptisms of public figures are based on two factors, according to Ryan Cragun, an associate professor of sociology who studies Mormonism at the University of Tampa. People naturally think about celebrities more often because they see them or hear about the frequently, and Mormons are similar to other social groups in that they like to claim famous people as their own.

Helen Radkey, who left the LDS Church in the 1970s and was later excommunicated for publicly criticizing it, dedicated countless hours to researching proxy baptisms. Radkey's research showed that in the span of five years, proxy baptisms were performed on at least twenty Holocaust victims, plus Humphrey Bogart, Marilyn Monroe, President Obama's late mother, Elvis Presley, Pope John Paul II, Joan of Arc, Gandhi, the grandparents of Carrie Fisher, Steven Spielberg, and Joe Biden, and the parents of Nazi-hunter Simon Wiesenthal. Radkey also uncovered attempts to baptize O.J. Simpson, Charles Manson, and mass shooters Stephen Paddock, and Devin Patrick Kelley. When Radkey shared her findings with the Associated Press, the LDS acknowledged the ceremonies violated its policy and said they would be invalidated, while also noting it had created safeguards to improve compliance. There are the rules, and then there is what people actually do. Controversies have erupted when new proxy baptisms were found in the church's database, including Radkey's 2012 discovery of one performed on Anne Frank. Add that to the *nine* proxy baptisms she received between 1989 and 1999. Perhaps with a mind for balance, the LDS did one for Adolf Hitler, too.

Joan of Arc, unwitting LDS member.

Chaotic Good

Similar and yet distinct from Mormon posthumous baptism is the "pink mass" of The Satanic Temple. The Satanic Temple, not to be confused with Anton LaVey's Church of Satan, is an atheistic organization founded in 2014, which prizes personal autonomy and uses Satan as a symbol of rebellion rather than a figure to be worshiped. Their central tenets include such things as "One should strive to act with compassion and empathy towards all creatures in accordance with reason." "One's body is inviolable, subject to one's own will alone." "Beliefs should conform to our best scientific understanding of the world." The Satanic Temple is the organization that made *The Satanic Children's Big Book of Activities* available to students in Florida after a Christian group was granted permission to hand out pamphlets and Bibles.

In July 2013, members of the Satanic Temple performed a pink mass over the grave of Catherine Idalette Johnston, the mother of Fred Phelps, Jr., founder of the reviled hate group the Westboro Baptist Church. The pink mass is a Satanic ritual that turns the deceased gay. The Satanic Temple turned the mother of the Westboro Baptist Church founder gay. That's not how that works exactly, but I like the way they think. There were actually two rituals performed over the headstone, both including readings and candle-lighting, one featuring two male Temple members kissing over the headstone, and the other with female members.

The idea came about after the Westboro Baptist Church had threatened to protest the funerals of victims of the Boston Marathon bombing. The Satanic Temple's website compared the pink mass to "the Mormon practice of baptizing the dead, only much gayer." "Upon completion of the pink mass ceremony, Catherine Johnston is now gay in the afterlife," notes the

Satanic Temple website, which has the cheeky URL www.westboro-baptist. com. "Fred Phelps is obligated to believe that his mother is now gay…[and] if beliefs are inviolable rights, nobody has the right to challenge our right to believe that Fred Phelps believes that his mother is now gay." Satanic Temple spokesperson, Lucien Greaves, who performed the ceremony said, "We intend to perform the pink mass for both Fred Phelps's father and great-aunt who raised him after his mother's death, but only in reply to their future pickets. The pink mass could be used to protest other anti-gay hysterics, but it is particularly appropriate when applied to Westboro."

CHAPTER 3

History

MIXED BAGS OF HISTORY

Before we dive into this topic, let me stress that the intent here is not to vilify or redeem anyone. People are what they are. For balance and to keep the mental pallet cleansed, we will alternate good and bad.

George Washington

Let's start with the first president of these United States. George Washington was said to have been so humble and noble that he refused a salary. However, he had an expense account that he downright exploited. In a seven-month period, Washington spent six thousand dollars, or the yearly salaries of seventy-five privates under his command, on booze. He used his expense account to lend money to friends who never paid him back and to buy extravagant things like a saddle that cost ten privates' salaries. At Valley Forge, one-sixth of the critically under-supplied colonial army died, many from starvation. The food situation was so desperate that Washington sent troops out to "forage," i.e., rob the nearby farms. Meanwhile, on his birthday, Washington ate mutton and hired a band. Bizarrely, to raise morale for the starving, often shoeless troops, Washington used his expense account to put on a play. That angered the Continental Congress to the point they banned the entire army from ever attending any play, on threat of court-martial. All told, Washington blew through over four million dollars in modern money.

Napoleon Bonaparte

In addition to being a brilliant general, Napoleon Bonaparte was a ruthless dictator, with no qualms against using force on French citizens, including ordering cannons to be used against protesters. At the same time, Napoleon governed his conquered territories under a system of laws based on equality. Titles acquired at birth were forbidden, which meant one's birth would not determine how good their future could be. Napoleon also set in motion a system of secular, public education reforms that would become the foundation for the modern educational system in much of Europe. He founded several state secondary schools to provide a standardized education open to everyone.

Napoleon: actually a little taller than average.

Abraham Lincoln

Ask any school child "Who freed the slaves?" and they will immediately yell "Abraham Lincoln!" We hold him up as a champion of humanity and equality.

His current reputation would surprise the audience of the famous debate with Senator Stephen Douglas, who heard Lincoln explain, "I am not, nor ever have been, in favor of bringing about in any way the social and political equality of the white and black races.... I am not nor ever have been in favor of making voters or jurors of Negroes, nor of qualifying them to hold office, nor to intermarry with white people.... There is a physical difference between the white and black races which I believe will forever forbid the two races from living together.... While they do remain together there must be a position of superior and inferior, and I as much as any other man am in favor of having the superior position assigned to the white race." Lincoln proposed relocating freed slaves to Liberia, Haiti, or Central America: anywhere but here.

> The Oregon territory outlawed slavery before it got statehood...and promptly outlawed all people of African descent in the territory, on pain of flogging every six months until they left.

Genghis Khan

Genghis Khan spread the Mongol Empire from China's Pacific coast to the doorstep of Europe, conquering or destroying small tribes and large cities. If riders of the Golden Horde appeared in the distance, it behooved you to surrender and pay tribute. If you resisted, you might be eradicated. Khan's empire killed 10 percent of the world's population, including two-thirds of northern China. If you did surrender, your life might actually improve. Not only were you allowed to continue practicing your faith, but Khan enforced religious equality. He upheld gender equality, with women seated as prominent advisers. Scholars, doctors, and skilled tradesmen were not only saved, but also encouraged to develop and teach their skills. Life could be so good in the khanate that some tribes sought out the Mongols, rather than waiting for the Mongols to reach them.

Mahatma Gandhi

Mahatma Gandhi's peaceful protests against the British rule of India have left an indelible mark on history. Gandhi was nominated for the Nobel Peace Prize five times. While he held firm to his principles of nonviolent resistance and poverty, his stance on celibacy...not so much. At age thirty-eight, he took a vow of *brahmacharya*, which means literally "living a spiritual life," but normally refers to chastity. Gandhi worked out a series of complex loopholes, which meant he could say he was technically chaste while still engaging in explicit sexual conversations and behavior. He routinely told married couples to take a cold bath when they felt sexual urges, while he carried on an affair with his physician for years. After the death of his wife, Gandhi gathered more and more women around him, whom he coaxed to sleep naked in his bed, including two eighteen-year-old grandnieces.

Al Capone

The top name in organized crime in the 1920s, Al Capone built a criminal empire that brought in $100 million a year. Crossing him was a fatal mistake, as seven men learned in a garage on Valentine's Day, 1929. Capone did not keep all that money for himself though. In 1931, Capone opened one of the nation's first soup kitchens, serving three thousand meals a day to men, women, and children who would otherwise go hungry.

Mother Teresa

Through the Order of the Missionaries of Charity, Teresa of Calcutta, a.k.a. Mother Teresa, devoted her life to helping the sick and impoverished of the world. From a distance, she looked like the pinnacle of Christian love, but saving souls may have been more important to her than saving lives. She saw the suffering of poverty as admirable, that it brought people closer to God. In the worst years, she condoned and even encouraged it in her hospitals and orphanages. Medical care was administered by volunteers with no training; staff could not distinguish the dying from the treatable; needles were reused until they were blunt; pain management was nonexistent. Mother Teresa told those in pain that they were being "kissed by Jesus," though she accepted the best medical care on her own deathbed.

Adolf Hitler

You knew that we could not get through this without talking about Adolf
Hitler, so I will make it quick. Hitler had it in for many types of people, chiefly
the children of Israel, but his list also included smokers. He ordered the first
public anti-smoking campaign in modern history. Hitler also passed laws to
stop experimentation on animals. Okay, that's enough.

Et Tu?

You would be disappointed to know how many of your childhood heroes
would have taken Hitler's side. In a 1983 interview, beloved author Roald
Dahl suggested that Hitler "didn't just pick on [the Jews] for no reason,"
adding that "there is a trait in the Jewish character that does provoke
animosity." Henry Ford was also grossly anti-Semitic. He bought the
Dearborn Independent newspaper to use as a platform for his unsavory
views; his insistence that Jews started World War I was even cited by Hitler
in *Mein Kampf*. Fashion designer Coco Chanel was a Nazi collaborator during
the occupation of France and helped fund anti-Semitic publications. Famed
aviator, Charles Lindbergh publicly claimed that Jews were trying to drag
America into the war through their ownership of the media. Walt Disney
supported a number of pro-Nazi organizations.

The latest trend? Antisemitism.

Saddam Hussein

Another world leader with a failing grade in all things humanitarian was Saddam Hussein. He ordered the deaths of thousands of Kurdish men, women, and children. At the same time, Hussein, like Napoleon, was a champion of education. Primary school enrollment was at 100 percent, and Hussein instituted a literacy program with the intent that the entire population of Iraq be able to read.

Winston Churchill

British Prime Minister, Winston Churchill's leadership during World War II helped lead the Allies to victory. He was not as universally loved as Americans might think. Churchill deliberately diverted food away from India during the war to feed Europeans, exacerbating one of the worst famines in the country's history, particularly in the state of Bengal. Some of India's grain was exported to Ceylon (now Sri Lanka) to meet needs there, even though Ceylon was in better condition than India. Australian wheat sailed past India to the Mediterranean and the Balkans. Offers of American and Canadian food aid were turned down. India was not permitted to use its own sterling reserves, or even its own ships, to import food. Because the British government paid inflated prices in the open market, grain became unaffordable for ordinary Indians. Churchill announced that Indians "must learn to look after themselves as we have done.... There is no reason why all parts of the British empire should not feel the pinch in the same way as the mother country has done." Churchill told the Secretary of State for India, "I hate Indians. They are a beastly people with a beastly religion." Three million Bengalis died of starvation.

A 2008 survey of British teenagers found that 23 percent thought Churchill was fictional, and 58 percent thought Sherlock Holmes was real.

Pablo Escobar

As history's biggest drug kingpin, Pablo Escobar was behind 80 percent of the world's cocaine traffic. With Escobar being responsible for over four thousand deaths, bombings, kidnappings, and political assassinations, it's hard to believe that anyone could have fond memories of him. The people in a neighborhood he built (and named after himself) do. In the 1980s, the government ignored the plight of the people in the Moravia neighborhood of Medellin, where 15,000 people were forced to live on a garbage dump the city had built. Escobar built a thousand new houses, a soccer field, and a sanitation system. He spent millions of dollars of his ill-gotten booty on more housing, seventy community soccer fields, and a zoo.

Great Balls of Scandal

Speaking of booty, pretty girls are part and parcel to the rock & roll lifestyle. For some, it was literally girls. Fresh off *Great Balls of Fire*, twenty-two-year-old Jerry Lee Lewis landed in England with a young girl on his arm, the daughter of his bass player/cousin, his new bride Myra, age thirteen. When a reporter asked who she was, Myra said she was Jerry Lee's wife, because no one told her to keep it a secret. As if that was not enough, Lewis was already married. The British press ran with that, the public was outraged, and the band was practically run out of the country. The scandal never left Lewis. Elvis Presley married Priscilla Beaulieu when she was eighteen, but he began dating her when she was fourteen and he was twenty-five. Ted Nugent deserves special recognition for adopting the seventeen-year-old girl he wanted to sleep with to avoid being charged with kidnapping. The father of rock & roll, Chuck Berry, was convicted in 1961 of transporting a fourteen-year-old across state lines for the purpose of sex.

Yakuza

After the devastating Japanese earthquake in 2011, the organized crime syndicate the Yakuza was among the first responders. Within days, they dispatched trucks filled with food, water, and blankets to the affected areas. In the first two weeks, they donated over $500,000 in relief supplies. According to their *ninkyo* code, others should never be left to suffer. During the 1995

Kobe earthquake, they were the first to get supplies to victims. They are notoriously reticent about their donations, refusing to talk to the press. Their intentions are so honorable that crime reporter Atsushi Mizoguchi praised them, despite the fact that he had been stabbed by Yakuza members, twice.

Ulysses S. Grant

Like Lincoln, President Grant was concerned that Blacks and whites could not live together peacefully. His solution was to buy the Dominican Republic, then known as Santo Domingo, and send all four million freed Blacks there. The Dominican Republic was on board with this idea, which may have something to do with Dominican President Buenaventura Baez personally being offered $100,000 in the annexation treaty. The treaty did not go through, of course. Also not a fan of Jews, when he was still a general, Grant tried to ban Jews from Kentucky, Tennessee, and Mississippi. He blamed them for, of all things, cotton smuggling. Grant's order, General Order #11 (1862), is the only example of a purely anti-Semitic action taken by the US government. Inexplicably, Grant still won the Jewish vote both times that he ran for president.

President Grant.

Hells Angels

If there is one group of people most of us would avoid, it's the Hells Angels. Biker gangs are often in the business of drugs, murder, and a host of other illegal activities, but they are not without benevolence. In 2014, members of the Hells Angels waited in line at a California Walmart for five days before Black Friday. Once inside, they purchased every single child's bicycle in the store and donated them to a local charity. They also run an annual toy drive.

W.E.B. Du Bois

Civil rights leader and prolific writer W.E.B. Du Bois was one of the best-known spokesmen for African American rights and cofounded the National Association for the Advancement of Colored People. Thus, it's strange to think that he took a five-month Nazi-funded trip to Germany in 1936, on the condition that Du Bois not criticize their treatment of Jews. When Du Bois returned to the US, he wrote that the German hatred of Jews "is a reasoned prejudice, or an economic fear." Du Bois shared many of the Nazi views on Jews, saying Hitler's dictatorship was necessary and that national socialism made sense. Du Bois would spend years backpedaling and defending himself in the press.

Black Panther Party

While the Black Panthers were often portrayed as a gang, their leadership saw the organization as a political movement. The Black Panther party started several community programs, including free health clinics in thirteen African American communities. In order to better nurture black children in disenfranchised communities, Black Panthers spent two hours each morning cooking breakfast for children before school. The party served around 20,000 meals a week. "We were showing love for our people," said former party member David Lemieux.

The *Black Panther* comic book character debuted less than a year before the Black Panther party emerged in 1966. In 1972, the publisher tried to change him to "Black Leopard" to distance the character from the political group, but the change only lasted a few months.

THEM'S BITING WORDS

There are few things quite as satisfying as having a sharp comeback or a scathing insult at precisely the right moment. Most of us instead experience l'*espirit de l'escalier*, or "the staircase wit," meaning you only think of the perfect response too late, after you have left the party and are already down the stairs. Luckily for the subjects of this section, that's not a feeling they experience often.

Heaven for the Climate, Hell for the Company

The best-known American humorist of all was Mark Twain. He wrote classic tales like *The Adventures of Tom Sawyer* and *A Connecticut Yankee in King Arthur's Court*. He also wrote scathing insults as cutting as they were adroit. Of Lilian Aldrich, wife of Thomas Bailey Aldrich, editor of *The Atlantic Monthly*, Twain said, "I do not believe I could learn to like her except on a raft at sea with no other provisions in sight." He reviewed J.M.W. Turner's painting *The Slave Ship* by saying, "It resembles a tortoise shell cat having a fit in a plate of tomatoes."

Fellow authors were an especial target for Twain's antipathy. "Once you've put one of [Henry James'] books down, you simply can't pick it up again." Of Scottish novelist and historian, Sir Walter Scott, Twain wrote, "He did measureless harm; more real and lasting harm, perhaps, than any other individual that ever wrote."

Twain had a profound dislike for the works of Jane Austen. In a letter to a friend, he said, "I haven't any right to criticize books, and I don't do it except when I hate them. I often want to criticize Jane Austen, but her books madden me so that I can't conceal my frenzy from the reader; and therefore I have to stop every time I begin. Every time I read *Pride and Prejudice*, I want to dig her up and beat her over the skull with her own shinbone." In another letter, Twain could not resist taking another shot at Austen as he and a friend discussed authors, "...to me his prose is unreadable—like Jane Austen's. No, there is a difference. I could read his prose on salary, but not Jane's. Jane is entirely impossible. It seems a great pity that they allowed her to die a natural death."

> Samuel Clemens' nom de plume Mark Twain is a measure of depth he learned while working on a river boat. The second knot on the weighted line dropped into the water was "mark twain" or two fathoms (twelve feet or 3.6 meters).

Beyond Twain's scorn, Henry James came under fire from his peers a great deal. "Henry James has a mind—a sensibility—so fine that no mere idea could ever penetrate it," said T. S. Eliot. William Faulkner called James "one of the nicest old ladies I ever met." H.G. Wells had a few things to say, describing James as "a hippopotamus trying to pick up a pea." "[A book by Henry James] is like a church lit but without a congregation to distract you, with every light and line focused on the high altar. And on the altar, very reverently placed, intensely there, is a dead kitten, an eggshell, a bit of string."

Brush My Teeth and Sharpen My Tongue

Dorothy Parker (1893–1967) was a famously wry, witty, and acerbic writer and critic. A fixture of 1920s literary society, she became a member of the famous Algonquin Round Table, a group of New York City critics, writers, and actors, including such greats as Groucho Marx, whose first gathering was part of a practical joke. Parker's sharp humor, low opinion of relationships, and general disdain made her a fascinating figure. Her wit was apparent from an early age. When her father remarried after her mother's death, she called her stepmother "the housekeeper."

When Parker was told that former President Calvin Coolidge, known as a man of few words, had died, she responded, "How could they tell?" Of the Yale prom, she said, "If all the girls attending it were laid end to end, I wouldn't be at all surprised." It was that saucy humor that got her fired from her job as a staff writer at *Vanity Fair*, after a wisecrack at the expense of an actress who was married to one of the magazine's biggest advertisers. Parker spoke openly about having had an abortion, a thing that simply was not done in the 1920s, saying, "It serves me right for putting all my eggs in one bastard." She was described by journalist and critic Alexander Woolcott as "a combination of Little Nell and Lady Macbeth."

The indomitable Dorothy Parker.

Working as a critic was a natural fit for Parker's cleverness. It afforded her the chance to be paid to say things like:

"The House Beautiful is, for me, the play lousy." (reviewing books for the *New York Times* under the pseudonym Constant Reader) "And it is that word 'hummy,' my darlings, that marks the first place in *The House at Pooh Corner* at which Tonstant Weader fwowed up"; "Katharine Hepburn delivered a striking performance that ran the gamut of emotions, from A to B," in the play *The Lake*; and of Benito Mussolini's *The Cardinal's Mistress*, "This is not a novel to be tossed aside lightly. It should be thrown with great force."

Parker clearly did not intend her humor to end with her life. Some of her proposed epitaphs included "Excuse my dust," and "Wherever she went, including here, it was against her better judgment."

Bipartisan Barbs

Insults are not exclusive to writers. Politics is also a fertile ground for barbs and jabs. Winston Churchill, prime minister of the United Kingdom during WWII, may have been responsible for international diplomacy, but was not known for censoring his opinions. Churchill was not a fan of Lady Jane Astor, an American-born woman who became the first female member of the British parliament; neither was she a fan of him. In one exchange, she said to Churchill, "If you were my husband, I'd put poison in your coffee." He responded, "Madam, if you were my wife, I'd drink it." His dealings were similar with Labour party politician Bessie Braddock, when she described him as being "disgustingly drunk." "My dear, you are ugly, and what's more, you are disgustingly ugly. But tomorrow I shall be sober, and you will still be disgustingly ugly."

Churchill was rarely more polite with his male contemporaries, even the ones in his own party, and especially those who were prime minister before and after him. Clement Attlee was, "a sheep in sheep's clothing," "a modest man with much to be modest about," and Churchill said that, "An empty cab pulled up to Downing Street. Clement Attlee got out." Stafford Cripps had, "all the virtues I dislike and none of the vices I admire." Of Stanley Baldwin, Churchill said, "He occasionally stumbled over the truth, but hastily picked himself up and hurried on as if nothing had happened." When Baldwin turned eighty, Churchill declined to send him a card, saying, "I wish Stanley Baldwin no ill, but it would have been much better if he had never lived." (Author George Orwell did not favor Baldwin any better, "One could not even dignify him with the name of stuffed shirt. He was simply a hole in the air.") Ramsay MacDonald had "a gift for compressing the largest amount of words into the smallest amount of thought." Neville Chamberlain's attempted appeasement of Nazi Germany earned him the declaration, "An appeaser is one who feeds a crocodile, hoping it will eat him last" and that Chamberlain "looked at foreign affairs through the wrong end of a municipal drainpipe." Regarding Charles de Gaulle of France, Britain's ally in the war, Churchill asked, "What can you do with a man who looks like a female llama surprised when bathing?" Of his Yankee confederates, Churchill thought, "You can always count on the Americans to do the right thing…after they've tried everything else." At least

Churchill knew where the worst of his vitriol should be aimed, describing Adolf Hitler as "a blood-thirsty guttersnipe, a monster of wickedness, insatiable in his lust for plunder and blood."

Four Score and a Few Burns

Another leader whose legacy was secured by war was Abraham Lincoln. A humble and unassuming man, his most-repeated quotes are folksy and practical. During one of the famous Lincoln-Douglas debates, for example, when accused of being two-faced, Lincoln calmly asked the audience, "If I had two faces, would I be wearing this one?" Less attention is paid to his more cutting turns of phrase. In another debate, Lincoln referred to Stephen Douglas's policy on slavery in the territories, "as thin as the homeopathic soup that was made by boiling the shadow of a pigeon that had starved to death." During the Civil War, Union General George B. McClellan repeatedly disappointed Lincoln with inaction, including refusing to attack Confederate General Robert E. Lee's troops in Richmond, VA. Lincoln wrote McClellan a one-sentence letter: "If you don't want to use the army, I should like to borrow it for a while." When McClellan's successor General Joseph Hooker sent a dispatch to the White House entitled "Headquarters in the Saddle," Lincoln quipped, "The trouble with Hooker is that he's got his headquarters where his hindquarters ought to be."

> The world of political insults and sports sometimes overlap. During the Great Depression, a reporter pointed out to Babe Ruth that he was earning more money than President Herbert Hoover. Ruth retorted, "Maybe so, but I had a better year than he did."

It's Hard to Be Humble

Talking trash is a key component of sports, especially boxing, and the king of pre-fight insults was Muhammad Ali. If a prize belt was awarded for braggadocio, Ali would have been the undisputed champion. "I'm so fast that last night I turned off the light switch in my hotel room and was in bed before the room was dark." "Float like a butterfly, sting like a bee" still pops up in TV and movies, though usually without the second half, "the hands can't hit what they eyes can't see." Many athletes boast, but Ali put his in rhyme. "I wrestled with an alligator, I tussled with a whale, I handcuffed lightning, thrown thunder in jail, I'm bad man.... Last week I murdered a rock, injured a stone, hospitalized a brick. I'm so mean I make medicine sick."

When legendary sportscaster Howard Cosell expressed doubt that Ali was still in good enough form to beat the younger George Foreman, Ali snapped back, "You're always talking about, 'Muhammad, you're not the same man you were ten years ago.' Well, I asked your wife and she says you aren't the same man you was two years ago." In that fight with Foreman, the famous 1974 "Rumble in the Jungle," Ali took everything Foreman had to offer for the first seven rounds. "Is that all you got, George?" Ali asked, winning by knockout in the eighth round. "I've seen George Foreman shadow boxing. And the shadow won."

President Jimmy Carter greets Muhammad Ali (Cassius Clay at the time) at a White House dinner celebrating the signing of the Panama Canal Treaty.

Ali's skill in the ring and larger-than-life personality meant that his legend has overshadowed some of the history of his career. Specifically, his brags and insults have survived, but often the identity of the competitor he said it to or about paled in comparison. Some of his "greatest hits" include:

- "If they can make penicillin out of moldy bread, they can sure make something out of you."

- "If you even dream about beating me, you better wake up and apologize!"

- "I'll beat him so bad; he'll need a shoehorn to put his hat on!"

- "Sonny Liston is nothing.... The man needs boxing lessons. And since he's gonna fight me, he needs falling lessons."

Ali's grandstanding style did not endear him with everyone. His response? "It's not bragging if you can back it up."

What Is It Good For?

Sports lends itself to bold words and posturing, but not nearly as well as warfare does. While the graphic novel and movie *300*, took some historic liberties with the story of King Leonidas I and his Spartan soldiers fighting valiantly against the far more numerous Persians at Thermopylae, it did accurately capture the Spartan spirit. In 480 BCE, King Xerxes of Persia sought to conquer the city-states of Greece. The Greek force of seven thousand men, of whom three hundred were Spartans, chose the narrow pass between the mountains at Thermopylae as the first line of defense. According to Plutarch, Xerxes demanded that the Spartans surrender their weapons. King Leonidas I responded, "*Molon labe*," which basically translates to "Come and take them." Xerxes did, as it turned out. The Greeks forces were wiped out, though the three-day battle bought time for the people of Athens to evacuate.

A monument to Leonidas I.

More than a century later, Philip II of Macedon, father of Alexander the Great, was also trying to conquer all of Greece. During the Third Sacred War, most city-states surrendered or were defeated. Not Sparta, though. Philip II sent threatening warnings to try to bring them to heel. "If I win this war, you will be slaves forever." In another, he vowed, "You are advised to submit without further delay, for if I bring my army on your land, I will destroy your farms, slay your people, and raze your city." King Cleomenes II of Sparta responded with a single word, "If." Philip II apparently decided attacking Sparta would have cost more than it was worth. Both he and Alexander the Great focused on the rest of the known world and avoided the only city-state without defensive walls.

Though Switzerland has been neutral since 1815, that did not equate to being helpless. The Alpine terrain formed a natural obstacle to invasion, and their direct democracy that meant their country could not be surrendered by any one leader, unlike nations with a king or dictator. Their citizens were armed with rifles and renowned for their skill as marksmen. To this day, every male citizen is required to attend recruit school and is trained on and issued a Fucile d'assalto selective fire rifle. When the German Kaiser Wilhelm II asked in 1912 what the quarter-million Swiss militiamen would do if invaded by a half-million German soldiers, a Swiss man whose identity is lost to time calmly replied, "Shoot twice and go home."

Jack Churchill, no relations to Winston, was a character worthy of an entire chapter. He charged into battle in WWII with a claymore sword and bagpipes and was the last Englishman to kill an enemy in war with a longbow. War suited him, so much so that when the war ended, he complained, "If it weren't for those damn Yanks, we could have kept the war going another ten years."

Lieutenant Colonel Ted Roosevelt III, son of President Theodore Roosevelt, served with distinction in WWI, showing *esprit de corps* with acts like buying proper boots for his men with his own money when the ones they were issued were insufficient. Despite being in his fifties, suffering from a heart condition and walking with a cane due to arthritis, Roosevelt served again in WWII, rising to Brigadier General. Assigned to help prepare the troops in England for the Normandy invasion, Roosevelt demanded to land on Utah Beach with his soldiers. Unfortunately, his men landed a mile off course. This was no bother to Roosevelt, who declared, "Then we'll start the war right here!"

Quit Stalin

Josip Broz Tito (1892–1980) was a Yugoslav revolutionary who rose to power to construct the "second Yugoslavia," a socialist federation that lasted from World War II until the fall of the Soviet Union in 1991. He was the first communist leader in power to defy centralized Soviet control, working instead for a form of socialism referred to as "national communism," and a proponent of noninvolvement in the Cold War. Soviet premier, Joseph Stalin tried to remove Tito repeatedly, through attempted purges of Yugoslav leadership, public condemnation, economic sanctions, and threats of military force. Officials in Moscow assumed that once it was common knowledge that Tito had lost Soviet approval, his power would evaporate. "I will shake my little finger and there will be no more Tito," Stalin remarked. Tito did not waver. Stalin ordered several assassination attempts on Tito, as was his custom, but none of them succeeded. In an official correspondence in 1949, Tito wrote to Stalin, "Stop sending people to kill me. We've already captured five of them, one of them with a bomb and another with a rifle.... If you don't stop sending killers, I'll send one to Moscow, and I won't have to send a second." Tito's threat seems to have worked. He would not die until 1980, of a septic infection in a Ljubljana hospital.

FIGHTING GIRLFRIEND AND THE NIGHT WITCHES

"A wife is not an instrument you can hang on the wall when you're tired of playing on it."[1]

—Russian proverb

---

1   There are lots of Russian proverbs about wives. That was the most flattering one I could find.

The Real Tank Girl

As many as 800,000 women served in Russia's Red Army during World War II. Unlike their sisters in England or America, they were much more likely to be fighting on the front lines than simply being in support roles. One woman, Mariya Oktyabrskaya, threw herself into the thick of the action. Mariya Vasilyevna was born in Crimea in August 1905 as a serf. That's the same kind of serf you learned about in history class, where people, like Mariya, her parents, and her nine siblings were subjects of a feudal lord. They lived in wrenching poverty and required the lord's permission for many things in their lives. It's little wonder that people flocked to the idea of communism as the Russian Empire gave way to the Soviet Union in 1922. The feudal system was gone and Mariya had the freedom to leave her family's farm for other jobs and to get an education.

In 1925, Mariya met and fell in love with Ilya Oktyabrskaya, a Soviet army officer. They married that same year, and Mariya quickly became fascinated all things military, saying in a letter to her sister, "Marry a serviceman and you serve in the army; an officer's wife is not only a proud woman, but also a responsible title." She joined the "Military Wives Council," trained as a nurse, was trained on a variety of weapons, and learned how to drive, which few women did at the time. The couple could not have children, but by all accounts they were happy together, until Ilya was sent to fight in what the Soviet Union called The Great Patriotic War and the rest of the world called World War II.

The war began badly for the Soviet Union. Adolf Hitler had made a nonaggression pact with Joseph Stalin to keep the Soviet Union out of the war. Two years later, however, Germany launched Operation Barbarossa, the largest invasion force in history, 3.8 million troops, 3,350 tanks, 2,770 planes, and 7,200 pieces of artillery. While some models of Soviet tanks were superior to Germans models, the Soviets did not have enough of them. They were also short on trucks, ammunition, radios, and other equipment, which gave the Germans an advantage.

When the eastern front of World War II opened, Oktyabrskaya was among those evacuated to Tomsk in Siberia. While trying to make the best of living there, she received the news that Ilya had been killed outside Kiev in August 1941. It had taken two years for the news to reach her. Oktyabrskaya did not respond to being widowed as most women would. She sold all her possessions to buy a T-34 medium tank to donate to the Red Army, writing directly to Joseph Stalin:

My husband was killed in action defending the motherland. I want revenge on the fascist dogs for his death and for the death of Soviet people tortured by the fascist barbarians. For this purpose, I've deposited all my personal savings—50,000 rubles—to the National Bank in order to build a tank. I kindly ask to name the tank "Fighting Girlfriend" and to send me to the frontline as a driver of said tank.

For reasons that will remain a mystery, Stalin agreed immediately. At age thirty-eight, Oktyabrskaya began five months of training with a highly skeptical tank squad. This was considerably more time than her male counterparts got; many of them were sent to the front unprepared. Oktyabrskaya, however, knew not only how to drive and operate Fighting Girlfriend, but how to repair her. In September 1943, she was assigned to the 26th Guards Tank Brigade as a driver and mechanic. Most of her comrades thought she was a publicity stunt or a joke, and they treated her as such.

A tank similar to the one Oktyabrskaya bought, operated, and repaired.

They would see they were wrong on October 1943, in Smolensk, 220 miles southwest of Moscow. The Germans had held the city for two years. While the Russians were able to reclaim most of it in September, there was still considerable German resistance. Oktyabrskaya and Fighting Girlfriend took out several anti-tank guns and machine gun nests. Fighting Girlfriend was hit; Oktyabrskaya jumped out under heavy fire and repaired the damage before rejoining the fight. In another letter to a sister, Oktyabrskaya wrote, "I've had my baptism by fire…. Sometimes, I'm so angry I can't even breathe." Oktyabrskaya was promoted to the rank of Sergeant, and the men of her unit began to call her "mother."

During an attack on a German defensive position in November, an artillery shell blew out Fighting Girlfriend's tracks, and Oktyabrskaya again jumped out to fix her tank, though this time she was given cover fire. On January 17, 1944, outside the town of Shvedy, Oktyabrskaya attacked several German machine gun nests and artillery guns, when Fighting Girlfriend was hit by a German anti-tank shell. As usual, Oktyabrskaya got out under fire to make repairs, but her luck did not hold. Another anti-tank shell exploded nearby, showering her with shrapnel, some of which hit her head. She lay in a coma for two months before finally rejoining her beloved Ilya. That August, Mariya Oktyabrskaya was declared a Hero of the Soviet Union.

Death from Above

Oktyabrskaya was certainly not the only Soviet woman to make a name for herself in the war effort with a vehicle. With outdated, under-powered planes, insufficient supplies, ill-fitting uniforms, and no respect from their male contemporaries, the 588th Night Bomber regiment still managed to strike such fear and hatred into the Nazis that any German airman who shot one down was awarded the Iron Cross medal. Their nickname, *Nachthexen*, "Night Witches," was given to them by their enemies, for the whooshing noise their wooden planes made as they dove, which the Nazis thought must have been what witches' brooms sounded like. The Night Witches dropped over 23,000 tons of bombs on German targets and proved themselves a crucial asset to the Soviet war effort.

Women had initially been banned from combat, but Soviet leaders were forced to rethink that policy under the massive pressure of Operation Barbarossa. In a few short months, Leningrad was under siege, Nazis were only a few miles away from Moscow, and the Red Army was struggling. The idea for an all-female squadron came from Marina Raskova, the "Soviet Amelia Earhart," who set numerous long-distance flying records and was the first woman to become a navigator in the Soviet Air Force and an instructor at the Zhukovsky Air Academy. Women across the Soviet Union, many of whom had lost loved ones in the war, wrote to her asking for her help to become pilots, but all that was available to them were support roles. Raskova petitioned Stalin to let her form a unit of female fighter pilots. Her request was granted in October 1941, when Stalin ordered the creation of not one, but three all-female air force units, making the Soviet Union the first WWII power to allow women in combat.

More than two thousand women applied, from which Raskova selected around four hundred, most of them students in their early twenties. Training took place at the Engels School of Aviation north of Stalin, where they were expected to learn in a few months what normally took years to teach. Each recruit had to be proficient as pilot, navigator, maintenance, and ground crew. They had to learn all this while dealing with near-constant derision and sexual harassment from men who believed that women could not possibly be useful in combat.

The female units were issued Polikarpov Po-2 biplanes, twenty-year-old crop-dusters. Male airmen used them in training, but the women were expected to use in combat. It would be a bit like being sent into a medieval battle with a wooden sword. Made of canvas stretched over plywood with an open cockpit, the Polikarpovs offered no protection from the blisteringly cold night wind. The planes were so light that gale force winds could blow them away, and the women had to lie on the wings to weigh them down during storms. There were no female uniforms, and even the smallest boots were still too big for them. Some women tore up their bedding to stuff in their boots, which had the added benefit of providing a little insulation. With military funding and the Polikarpovs' weight capacity both being limited, the women had to make do without radar, radios, or defensive guns. They were given the most basic tools, like rulers, stopwatches, flashlights, paper maps, and compasses. If they were hit by incendiary tracer rounds, their planes would burst into flames. They were also not issued parachutes. The weight of the bombs, one under each wing, forced them to fly at lower altitudes, which is why they only flew at night. The Night Witches' only defense from enemy fire would be to put their planes into a dive.

A 1969 stamp commemorating the Po-2.

Some of the Polikarpovs' shortcomings turned out to be blessings in disguise. Their maximum speed of 94 mph (or 151 kmph) was slower than the stall speed of the Nazi planes. They were highly maneuverable, making them hard to target. They could also easily take off and land from locations that more modern planes could not. The planes were too small to show up on radar and, not having radios, could not be picked up by radio locators.

The Night Witches practiced "harassment bombing," targeting camps, supply depots, rear base areas, etc. The constant raids gave the enemy little time to rest and kept them under duress. Each night, as many as forty crews, pilot up front and navigator behind, would run eight to eighteen missions, flying back between runs to rearm. Two planes would go out, almost as bait, attracting German spotlights to give them enough light to see. They would split off suddenly, and the German spotlights and flak guns would struggle to target them. While that was happening, a third last plane would cut its engines and glide in to bomb the target, making the witch's broom sound that was the only warning the Nazis had. By the time they heard it, it would be too late. Like Mariya Oktyabrskaya repairing Fighting Girlfriend under fire, the Night Witches would have to climb out of the cockpit to restart the engine manually so they could escape.

Night Witches created their own list of commandments, starting with "Be proud you are a woman." Though they were proficient in killing their enemies while enduring terrible conditions, they enjoyed dancing, needlework, and decorating their planes during their downtime. They even used their navigation pencils as eyeliner.

Their last flight took place on May 4, 1945, three days before Germany officially surrendered. The Night Witches flew more than eight hundred runs per crew. Amazingly, given what they had to work with, they only lost thirty pilots. Twenty-four Night Witches, including Raskova, were awarded the title of Hero of the Soviet Union. Raskova, who died on January 4, 1943, was given the first state funeral of World War II, and her ashes were buried in the Kremlin.

Despite being the most highly decorated unit in the Soviet Air Force, the Night Witches were disbanded. They were also excluded from the official victory parade in Moscow, ostensibly, because their planes were too slow.

CHAPTER 4

The Arts

READ A RAINBOW

I'm in the Book

Considering that there have probably been more "yellow pages" phone books in print than any other publication in history, it's odd to think that they fell out of use in the span of a few years. The first phone directory was created in 1878 on a single piece of card stock, with fifty listings and no numbers. It only listed the names of the businesses that owned a telephone, since human operators connected all the calls. In 1880, a British telephone directory had a whopping 248 listings. According to legend, yellow phone books started in 1883, when a printer in Wyoming ran out of white paper and substituted yellow, and the practice stuck. Early phone books included directions for using the telephone, since people were prone to talking into the wrong part. For an item that was once so ubiquitous, it's surprisingly hard to find early examples. There was no compelling reason to save them and phone companies would pick up last year's when they brought you this year's. You may wish your grandparents had kept theirs—one of the earliest phone books sold at auction for $170,000.

> The telephone taught us to greet people with "hello." "Hello" had existed in English for hundreds of years, but it was an exclamation, as in "Hello, what have we here?" Alexander Graham Bell wanted people to say "Ahoy."

Whereas big companies usually patent, trademark, and copyright every little thing they create, AT&T did not apply for intellectual property protection for the phrase "yellow pages" or the original walking fingers logo, created in 1962. That meant other publishers could use them freely. In many countries, "yellow pages," or the local translation, *are* registered trademarks of their local owner, usually the main national telephone company. Speaking of intellectual property rights, in 1991, the Supreme Court declared that directory listings could not be copyrighted, because the mere accumulation of information required no creative expression.

Be honest, when's the last time you cracked one of these open?

Google: The Analog Years

Apart from color, and the fact that one is business and the other is people, an important distinction between the yellow pages and the white pages is that the Telecommunications Act of 1996 allows any publisher to print the yellow pages, but the white pages can only come from the phone company. In some areas, you might get half a dozen different yellow pages each year. The yellow pages remain a fourteen billion dollar a year industry, which is why people are still interested in printing it. 540 million directories are printed in the United States each year, about 1.7 directories per person. With the average yellow pages book weighing 3.6 pounds (or 1.6 kilograms), that means two billion pounds of paper, or twenty-three million trees, are used to make these books. Though the physical books are falling out of use, the yellow pages are still profitable thanks to the shift to online advertising. (Personally, the only people I know who use phone books are sideshow strongmen. The trick is to fan the pages out first.)

As Good As...

The Poky Little Puppy, The Ugly Duckling, Scruffy the Tugboat, and *Mother Goose* do not have colors in their names, but they are all golden. These beloved titles are Little Golden Books, created in 1942 through a partnership between publisher Simon & Schuster, the Artists and Writers Guild, and the

Western Printing and Lithographing Company. In the early 1940s, children's books cost the equivalent of thirty dollars, too expensive for many families. George Duplaix, head of the Artists and Writers Guild, wanted to make reading more accessible. He set out to develop sturdy, illustrated children's books that would be affordable to most families with young children. The group decided to publish twelve titles for simultaneous release in what would be called the Little Golden Books Series. Each staple-bound book would have forty-two pages, twenty-eight printed in two colors, and fourteen in four colors. The group calculated that if the print run for each title was 50,000 copies, the books could affordably be sold for twenty-five cents each, equivalent to their price now.

The first Little Golden Books published were *Three Little Kittens*, *The Little Red Hen*, and *The Alphabet from A to Z*. Early editors worked with educators and psychologists to determine what children cared about and which story lines would appeal to readers. The books reflected a shift in thinking about how, where, and what children should read. The books were sold in places children and families already shopped, like department stores and drugstores. A small town may not have a bookstore, but it would have a five-and-dime. There were no author or illustrator credits on the covers, only a colorful illustration and the title. The distinctive gold binding of Little Golden Books and the trim size, designed to fit in a child's hands, were early examples of branding in children's books. Five months after they launched, the publisher had printed 1.5 million copies.

Of the dozen titles that debuted in 1942, only *The Poky Little Puppy* was an original story; the rest were classic tales and nursery rhymes. *The Poky Little Puppy* is cited as the bestselling children's hardcover book of all time. Over 1,400 Little Golden Books titles have been published, including Bible stories and pop culture tie-ins, like Star Wars and Barbie. The price of the Little Golden Books titles rose with inflation through the years (twenty-nine cents in 1962, fifty-nine cents in 1977, ninety-nine cents in 1986, etc.), currently selling for three to five dollars. There is also a lucrative seller's market for first editions and other rare versions. A 1942 version of *Mother Goose* with the original dust jacket can be yours from a specialty bookseller for a mere $1,375.

Vacation During Segregation

The color green gets the hat-trick, with a lifesaving travel guide, a censorship manual, and a dictator's manifesto. "There will be a day sometime in the near future when this guide will not have to be published. That is when we as a race will have equal opportunities and privileges in the United States. It will be a great day for us to suspend this publication for then we can go wherever we please and without embarrassment." This was opening of *The Negro Motorist Green Book*, first published in 1936. It provided listings of hotels, guest houses, service stations, drug stores, taverns, barber shops, and restaurants that would serve and be safe for African American travelers. The *Green Book* focused on segregationist strongholds like Alabama and Mississippi, but its coverage extended from Connecticut to California. With Jim Crow still looming over much of the country, the motto on the guide's cover doubled as a warning: "Carry your *Green Book* with you. You may need it."

Rates of car ownership exploded after World War II, but the great American road trip was fraught with risk for African Americans. "Whites only" policies meant that many black travelers packed all the food they thought they would need, for fear of being unable to find a restaurant that would serve them, as well as being prepared to sleep in their car every night. So-called "sundown towns," municipalities that banned Blacks after dark, were scattered across the country. The *Green Book* was the brainchild of Harlem postal carrier Victor Hugo Green, who took inspiration from similar guides for Jewish travelers. Like most African Americans in the mid-twentieth century, Green had grown weary of the discrimination people of color faced whenever they ventured outside their neighborhoods. The first *Green Book* only covered hotels and restaurants in New York City, but Green soon expanded its scope, using fellow postal carriers as scouts and paying cash to readers who sent in information. By the early 1940s, the *Green Book* boasted thousands of listings across the country, all of them black-owned or verified to be integrated. In cities with no black-friendly hotels, the book listed the addresses of homeowners willing to rent rooms, a sort of early Airbnb.

"The *Green Book* was the Bible of every Negro highway traveler in the 1950s and early 1960s," wrote Earl Hutchinson Sr. in *A Colored Man's Journey*

Through 20th Century Segregated America. "You literally didn't dare leave home without it." Thanks to sponsorship from Standard Oil, the *Green Book* was available for purchase at Esso gas stations across the country. Though largely unknown to whites, it sold upwards of 15,000 copies per year. Later editions included information on airline and cruise ship travel to Canada, Mexico, the Caribbean, Africa, and Europe. In one of its last editions in 1963–64, it included a "Your Rights, Briefly Speaking" feature that listed state laws related to discrimination in travel accommodations. "The Negro is only demanding what everyone else wants," the article stressed, "what is guaranteed all citizens by the Constitution of the United States."

Victor Hugo Green did not live to see his book become obsolete, passing away in 1960. In 1964, the Civil Rights Act finally banned racial segregation in restaurants, theaters, hotels, parks, and other public places. Two years later, the Green Book quietly ceased publication.

Stiff Upper Lip

1949's *BBC Variety Programmes Policy Guide for Writers and Producers*, commonly referred to as the "green book," detailed what was then permissible as comedy material. Even as it tried to police comedians, which is never advisable, its bureaucratic tone and outlandish restrictions became comedy fodder in and of itself. The green book was created after an incident in 1944, when variety star Max Miller, master of double entendre, told an unscripted joke about a girl, a mountain pass, and a blocked passage. Miler found himself banned from the airwaves for five years.

Among jokes banned by the BBC's green book were those referencing lavatories, effeminacy in men, immorality of any kind, suggestive references to honeymoon couples, chambermaids, and the vulgar use of words such as "basket," the Polari word for a man's trouser bulge. Also forbidden were jokes that used a regional accent to make an innocuous statement sound dirty. For example, making "winter draws on" sound like "with her drawers on" was forbidden under the prohibition against mentioning ladies' undergarments. You could not even say "fig leaves" in reference to the bathing suit area.

Ahead of their time in one respect, many of the guidelines comply with modern notions of political correctness. No offense was to be given to other races. Derogatory references to the working class in general, miners specifically, and solicitors (i.e., lawyers) were out. The n-word was banned, though the phrase "N**** Minstrels" was inexplicably tolerated. You could only make a scant few jokes about drinking in any given program and "remarks such as 'one for the road' are inadmissible on road safety grounds." Some of the rules were quite specific. If a comedian wished to impersonate a real person, that person's permission was required. If that real person was dead, permission had to be obtained from the person's relatives. The most specific rule of all was the banning of any reference to the McGillycuddy of the Reeks, the last in a line of noble Irish chieftains, after he lodged complaints. It has been said, though, that the strictness of the rules unintentionally helped sharpen the writers' skills at crafting innuendos, having set them a challenge to get their jokes on their air.

Libyan Library

Less amusing than even the worst British comedy—including the 1990 sitcom about Hitler and his Jewish neighbors called *Heil, Honey, I'm Home*—was the "green book" of Libyan dictator, Muammar Qaddafi. First published in 1975, six years after Qaddafi seized power in al-Fateh Revolution, the book, actually entitled *Al-Kitab al-Akhdar*, was "intended to be read by all people." This was not a suggestion.

Some scholars have compared the Green Book's political and economic ideology to Rousseau, Mao, and Marx. There are precious few external sources cited, not even religious texts. "Most analyses of the Green Book emphasize Qaddafi's many digressions and penchant for stating the obvious, like his proclamation that 'woman is a female and man is a male,' " says *NY Times* reporter Mohamad Bazzi. The Green Book presented its own peculiar logic—a mixture of utopian socialism, Arab nationalism, and the Third World revolutionary ideology that was in vogue at the time, in a tone and style similar to classical Arabic literature. On the subject of gender, Qaddafi said men are aggressive by nature and "a woman is tender; a woman weeps easily and is easily frightened." This makes his forty virgin female bodyguards seem odd, as well as his decisions to arm and train the women of Tripoli.

Qaddafi's Green Book came in two volumes. In the first, *The Solution of the Problem of Democracy*, Qaddafi promised to rescue the world from the failures of Western democracy and communism. His "Third Universal Theory" would usher in an era in which people would rule themselves directly, without elections, political parties, or parliamentary representation. That sounds nice until you remember that people protesting Qaddafi were killed. The second volume offers *The Solution of the Economic Problem*. In some parts, Qaddafi appears to be a class-conscious self-help guru: "There are no wage-workers in the socialist society, only partners." In others, he exalts property ownership: "There is no freedom for a man who lives in another's house, whether he pays rent or not." Qaddafi venerated traditional tribal cultures, believing that stationary people were weak and inferior to nomadic people.

Libyan children spent two hours a week studying the Green Book. Extracts were broadcast daily on television and radio. Slogans from the book were plastered on billboards and painted on buildings. The World Center for the Study and Research of the Green Book had a staff of more than a hundred, and branches around the world. Through the 1980s and 1990s, the Center had a multi-million-dollar budget to translate the book into more than thirty languages, host international conferences, and fund studies and papers on Qaddafi's theories.

When Benghazi fell to rebel control at the beginning of the Libyan conflict, the Center was one of the first buildings to be attacked. Many copies of the book were burned during the conflict, and since Qaddafi's death, booksellers can't give copies away.

There are over 110 different acceptable ways to spell Muammar Qaddafi. Good luck with your spell-check.

The Party Line

Color-coded mandatory reading was also part of the Cultural Revolution in China. The "little red book," or *Quotations from Chairman Mao Zedong*, contained 267 aphorisms from the communist Chinese leader, covering subjects like class struggle, "correcting mistaken ideas" and the "mass line," a key tenet of Mao Zedong Thought. Included is Mao's famous remark that "political power grows out of the barrel of a gun." It was widely circulated in China and around the world during the Cultural Revolution (1966–1976). Originally produced in 1964 by the People's Liberation Army, it was a key feature of Mao's cult of personality. The Ministry of Culture aimed to distribute a copy to every Chinese citizen, and hundreds of new printing houses were built to achieve this. By the time the Chinese Communist Party ordered a halt to the printing of the book in February 1979, at least one billion official copies had been printed. Some estimates put the worldwide total as high as five billion copies, making it one of the most popular publications of the twentieth century.

A statue commemorating Chairman Mao.

The book was the brainchild of Lin Biao, a decorated general of the Chinese People's Liberation Army and Mao's right-hand man, for about a year. (People did not last long in the job before dying or disappearing.) Hoping to further his political ambitions, Biao asked the staff of the *People's Liberation Army Daily* to compile a small collection of Mao's quotations. Once the book was approved, a free copy was issued to every soldier, most of whom, like their fellow citizens, had little education and found it difficult to read. The aphorisms were offered without context and strung together without regard for chronology. The little red book soon became a political Bible and a source of spiritual inspiration. Every person in China had at least one copy, and reading and reciting it became a daily ritual.

During the 1960s, the book was the most visible icon in China, even more visible than the image of Mao himself. In posters created by communist propaganda artists, nearly every painted figure was seen with a copy of the book in their hand. The book was used during the Cultural Revolution not only to streamline ideology, but as a weapon against "class enemies" or "counter-revolutionaries." Owning and knowing the book "became a way of surviving," says Daniel Leese, professor of modern Chinese history and politics at the University of Freiburg. Paramilitary Red Guards, usually students mobilized to purify the Communist Party, would check whether those suspected of bourgeois tendencies were carrying the little red book and could quote from it. The Red Guard also used the book to accuse their own teachers and, eventually each other, of betraying Maoist values.

Millions of copies have published in translation and sold abroad. It was taken up by Western groups like the Black Panthers. Copies were passed around Warsaw Pact nations after the USSR's split from China ensured it would be banned. After the end of the Cultural Revolution in 1976 and the rise of Deng Xiaoping in 1978, the importance of the book waned considerably, as did the value of Mao's quotations. Today, *Quotations from Chairman Mao Zedong* is mostly a piece of nostalgia, available for purchase at tourist destinations. Certain editions are popular with collectors, and rare or unusual printings command high prices. There was even a spike in sales in the UK in 2015, when a member of parliament used it as a prop in a speech.

TO BOLDLY GO WHERE ONLY WHITE MEN HAD GONE BEFORE

Octavia Estelle Butler was born in 1947 to a housekeeper mother and shoe-shiner father who died when she was seven. Butler's mother raised her with the help of her own mother in a strict Baptist household. Because Butler's mother received little formal education herself, she made sure that her daughter was given the opportunity to learn by bringing home books and magazines that her white employers threw away. A shy only child, awkwardly tall and a target for bullies, Butler found solace in reading at the library and in writing. Though Butler's mother bought her a typewriter, it was in the hope that Butler would grow up to work as a secretary. Neither mother nor grandmother encouraged Butler's burgeoning love of writing. In their minds, and in the minds of many people of that era, women and people of color could not be professional writers.

Sitting in front of the low-budget movie *Devil Girl from Mars*, Butler, then twelve years old, said to herself, "Someone got paid for writing this story. I can write a better story than that!" Butler began reading science fiction at a young age, but she soon found the genre's unimaginative portrayal of ethnicity and class, as well as its lack of noteworthy female protagonists, disappointing.

An avid reader, Butler prevailed in her education. She graduated from Pasadena City College in 1968, her college years coming during the rising Black Power movement. Listening to classmates criticize the "subservience" of previous generations of Blacks to whites, Butler thought of her mother and felt empathy for her forebears rather than judgment. She supported herself with unskilled factory jobs and other mentally untaxing work that left her mind free to work on the stories that she would write for a few hours each morning. While participating in a local writer's workshop, Butler was encouraged to attend the Screen Writers Guild Open Door Program. There, she found a mentor in celebrated science fiction author Harlan Ellison, who was impressed by her writing. He urged her to attend the six-week Clarion Science Fiction Writers Workshop in Clarion, Pennsylvania. Butler sold her first stories soon after. "Crossover" was published in the 1971 Clarion anthology, and "Childfinder" was purchased by Ellison for an anthology that was never published. The Clarion Workshop was also where Butler met and became lifelong friends with multi-Nebula and Hugo Award-winning author Samuel R. Delaney.

Butler's alma mater today.

From 1976 to 1984, Butler worked on the novels that would become known as the Patternist series: *Patternmaster*, *Mind of My Mind*, *Survivor*, *Wild Seed*, and *Clay's Ark*. The series explored themes of what it means to be human, racial and gender-based animosity, the ethical implications of biological engineering, and how power changes people, through a secret history spanning from ancient Egypt to the far future, involving an alien pandemic and telepathic mind control. A major through-line of this series, and Butler's work as a whole, is the struggle of people of different lifestyles trying to coexist when one lifestyle has been labeled subversive, transgressive, or simply wrong. In Consuela Francis' 2009 *Conversations with Octavia Butler*, Butler said, "I see science fiction as a way of disseminating the fact that we don't have only one kind of people, namely white males, in the world. They are not the only ones who are here, not the only ones who count."

In 1978, a scant seven years after selling her first story, Butler was able to stop working and support herself as a writer. She paused the Patternist series to write 1979's *Kindred*, which told the story of a black woman who is transported from 1976 to 1815, where she is assumed to be an escaped slave and treated accordingly. While many were quick to categorize the book as science fiction because it involved time-travel, Butler herself referred to it as "a kind of grim fantasy" and pointed out that the science behind the time-travel is effectively ignored. While Butler enjoyed science fiction as both a reader and a writer, calling it "potentially the freest genre in existence," she resisted the label of "genre writer." Many call her work "literary science fiction" or "speculative fiction," a more nebulously defined genre that deals with the future without focusing on technology, like Margaret Atwood's *The Handmaid's Tale* or Robert Heinlein's *Stranger in a Strange Land*. Butler claimed to have three loyal audiences, from varied ethnic and cultural backgrounds: people of color, fans of science fiction, and feminists.

Butler's short story "Speech Sounds" won the Hugo Award for Short Story in 1984, which was a mere appetizer for 1985, when her novelette *Bloodchild* won the Hugo Award, the Locus Award, and the Science Fiction Chronicle Reader Award for Best Novelette. *Bloodchild* tells the story of humans on an alien world, who are protected by insect-like aliens that use the humans as hosts for breeding their young. This was also the period where Butler traveled to South America to research the Amazon rainforest and the Andes mountains for what would become the Xenogenesis trilogy: *Dawn, Adulthood Rite*, and *Imago*, publishing one book per year. Xenogenesis also examines humans coexisting, cooperating, and conflicting with an alien species, after a nuclear apocalypse destroys the world and mankind must merge their DNA with the aliens to survive in some form. Where *Kindred* was light on science fact, Xenogenesis depends on explanations of human anatomy and molecular biology. (Xenogenesis is now published as Lilith's Brood.) During the 1990s, Butler worked on the novels that further solidified her renown as an author: *Parable of the Sower* and *Parable of the Talents*. In 1995, she became the first science fiction writer to be awarded the John D. and Catherine T. MacArthur Foundation "genius grant" fellowship.

Butler experimented with alien contact, gene manipulation, contamination, hybridity, and nonconsensual breeding to shape characters built by sociobiological violence. The futuristic communities she created drew on African culture and the black experience in the diaspora of America. That is why she is called "the queen of Afrofuturism." The term "Afrofuturism" generally refers to literature, music, movies, and visual art that explores the African American experience through science fiction, how the culture intersects with technology and futurism. Coined by science fiction writer Samuel R. Delany in a 1995 interview, the purpose of the term is to set apart "speculative fiction that treats African American themes and addresses African American concerns in the context of twentieth century techno-culture—and, more generally, African American signification that appropriates images of technology and a prosthetically enhanced future.... African American voices have other stories to tell about culture, technology, and things to come." Marvel's *Black Panther* comics and movie, the works of artist Jean-Michele Basquiat, and even the musical *The Wiz* stand as examples of Afrofuturism.

Against a backdrop of fully realized science, Butler created tableaus of people who are often excluded from popular culture and minimized when history is recorded. "She had a deep commitment to science fiction," wrote mystery author Walter Mosley, a contemporary and friend of Butler's, "but her talent was in world-building. And underneath that was a social and political fever which spoke so loudly and clearly to women in the black community." The struggles of Butler's characters are timelessly relatable, which means that each new generation of readers can, and should, explore Butler's catalog. Her political and social themes speak particularly to activists. In the words of Butler's biographer, Ayana Jamieson, "People on the margins—Black people, women, science fiction readers, feminists, queer folks, variously abled and gendered folks—find parts of themselves in her work. Many of her works are coming-of-age tales where people are testing out and discovering who they are. That transformational process, along with the growing pains, joys, and shock that go along with it, really grabs people." Jamieson is also the founder of the Octavia Butler E. Legacy Network, whose mission is "to preserve and promote research and scholarship on one of the preeminent science fiction and fantasy writers of the twentieth century."

Octavia Butler died suddenly outside her home of a possible stroke and a fall in 2006 at age fifty-eight. However, the themes of her works—humanity's natural tendency toward oppression, overcoming disenfranchisement, embracing change to survive—are timeless. "Simple peck-order bullying,"

Butler wrote in the essay "A World without Racism," "is only the beginning of the kind of hierarchical behavior that can lead to racism, sexism, ethnocentrism, classism, and all the other 'isms' that cause so much suffering in the world." Butler's legacy is self-evident. Authors like Rivers Solomon, Karen Joy Fowler, Nalo Hopkinson, Nisi Shawl, Lester Spence, Valjeanne Jeffers, and K. Tempest Bradford cite her as influence and inspiration. Janelle Monae, the gender-bending, assumption-shattering singer who is credited as a force in Afrofuturism, said of Butler's work, "*Wild Seed* was the book that inspired me. I loved the characters, and the morphing. [Anyanwu] was just such a transformative character, and I look at myself as a transformative artist. Just the fact that [Butler] defied race and gender. You appreciated her work for being a human being."

LIGHTS, CURSES, ACTION!

Making a movie is a difficult, time-consuming, and expensive proposition. While some projects come together naturally, others seem to have tragedy, misfortune, and plain old bad luck heaped upon them.

"It's All for You, Damien!"

Horror films are fertile ground for apparent curses, and a movie would be hard-pressed to seem more cursed than 1976's *The Omen*, the tale of an American diplomat in Europe who adopts a baby boy, ostensibly the Antichrist, and people around him begin dying. Even Robert Munger, who came up with the concept for the film, began to feel uneasy during pre-production, telling producer Harvey Bernhard, "The Devil's greatest single weapon is to be invisible, and you're going to take off his cloak of invisibility to millions of people." Releasing the movie on June 6, 1976, as close as they could get to 666, probably did not help matters.

Gregory Peck had only recently agreed to play the role of the ambassador when his son shot and killed himself, leaving no suicide note. Undeterred, or perhaps therapeutically focusing on his work, Peck flew to England to begin filming. While flying through a storm over the Atlantic, Peck's plane was struck by lightning, causing an engine to catch fire and nearly causing them to crash into the ocean. The film's other producer, Mace Neufeld, also had his plane struck by lightning. Even after those long odds, that was not the end of their aerial adversity. One of the first shots planned for the film was an aerial overview of London, to be shot from a rented plane. At the last minute, the rental company gave the original plane to a group of Japanese businessmen instead. The curse did not seem to get that update, because that plane crashed, killing everyone on board.

One scene called for Peck to be attacked by "devil dogs," in the form of a pack of rottweilers. The dogs were supposed to attack a heavily padded stuntman. For reasons unknown, the dogs began to attack the stuntman in earnest, biting through the padding and ignoring their trainer's orders to stop. Another animal-based scene saw the big cat wrangler mauled to death by a tiger.

As if being in a plane struck by lightning was not harrowing enough, the Hilton hotel Neufeld was staying at exploded. Luckily, Neufeld was not there at the time. Not to be deterred, the curse turned its sights to the restaurant where the producers and other film executives were going, and it blew up, too. Neufeld missed the explosion by minutes. The perpetrator would turn out to be the Irish Republican Army, and it was only Neufeld's dodgy luck that he was meant to be in both places.

Special effects consultant John Richardson created *The Omen*'s unforgettable death scenes, including one in which a man is beheaded by a sheet of glass sailing off a runaway truck. Two weeks before the film was released, Richardson and his assistant, Liz Moore, were involved in a head-on collision. Moore was killed, cut in half by the other vehicle's wheel. Richardson opened his eyes after the collision to see a kilometer marker reading "Ommen 6,66," The closest town was Ommen, Netherlands, and the accident happened at kilometer 66.6.

Central Casting Out the Demon

The highest-grossing horror movie of all time, when adjusted for inflation, and the first horror movie to be nominated for the Oscar for Best Picture was

1973's *The Exorcist*. In it, a young girl named Reagan, played by Linda Blair, is possessed by a demon and forced to commit horrible acts as two priests fight to save her. The trouble started before filming even began, when the set caught fire, destroying everything except Reagan's room. The arsonist had talons, black, beady eyes, and was a harbinger of disease—a pigeon had somehow gotten into a circuit box, which caused a short that caused the fire. Reverend Thomas Bermingham, the technical adviser on the film, was asked to exorcise the set, but he refused.

Arsonists come in many forms.

Both Blair and Ellen Burstyn, who played her mother, were badly injured during the shoot. One scene had the demon violently throwing Reagan around on her bed. The rig the film crew used to create the convulsive movements broke during one take, injuring Blair's back. Another scene called for the demon to throw Burstyn across the room and into a wall, which the crew achieved with a wire rig. Director William Friedkin was unhappy with the first take and told the crewman operating the rig to use more force. He did not warn Burstyn. Her cry of alarm and pain in the film is genuine. Colliding with the wall at speed injured her lower spine, leaving her in permanent pain.

They were comparatively lucky. Actors Jack MacGowran and Vasiliki Maliaros, whose characters die in the movie, both died while it was in post-production. At least four other people, including a night watchman, died during filming. Max Von Sydow's brother died on Sydow's first day on set. Actress Mercedes McCambridge, who provided the voice of the demon Pazuzu, had to face a monumental tragedy when her son murdered his wife and children before committing suicide.

Many believed that the physical copies of the film were cursed and that showing it in a theater was an open invitation to evil. A church across the street from an Italian theater was struck by lightning during a showing. One movie-goer was so frightened they passed out in the theater and broke their jaw on the seat in front of them. They sued the filmmakers, claiming that subliminal messages in the film had caused them to faint. Warner Brothers settled out of court for an undisclosed amount. Not everything bad can be blamed on demons, though. People sent thirteen-year-old Blair so many death threats that the studio had to provide her with bodyguards for six months after the movie came out.

Speaking of demonic possession, the 2012 movie *The Possession* centers on a young girl who falls under the control of a malevolent spirit that lives inside an antique box called a dybbuk and is based on an alleged true story. Even though director Sam Raimi would not let the dybbuk box's owner bring it anywhere near the set, strange and frightening things started happening. Lights exploded directly over people's heads, strange smells and cold air blew in from nowhere, and, immediately after filming wrapped, all the props were destroyed in a fire; the fire department could not determine the cause.

Whatever Happened To...

Sometimes, a movie's bad karma takes time to manifest, and the misfortunes only crop up after the film is released. Horror classic *Rosemary's Baby*, released in the summer of 1968, was based on the premise that God is dead, but the Devil is alive and returning to Earth with the aid of a cult. The film's composer, Krzysztof Komeda, fell off a rock ledge at a party that fall. He lingered in a coma for four months before finally dying. His death was quite similar to the way the witches in the movie rid themselves of a suspicious friend of the titular Rosemary. The producer, William Castle, already suffering considerable stress from the amount of hate mail he had received about the film, was incapacitated with severe kidney stones. While delirious in the hospital, he cried out, "Rosemary, for God's sake, drop the knife!" Castle recovered his health but never made a successful movie again. Director Roman Polanski suffered no physical harm after the film. The same could not be said for his heavily pregnant wife, Sharon Tate. She and four friends were brutally murdered by members of the cult known as the Manson Family while *Rosemary's Baby* was still in theaters. In his autobiography, Polanski recalled he had had a "grotesque thought" the last time he saw his wife: "You will never see her again."

Conspiracy theorists and other nontraditional thinkers believe these events were set in motion by an elaborate Satanic plot at the behest of the Beatles. Their *White Album* was written at an Indian meditation retreat, which the movie's star, Mia Farrow, attended. The song title "Helter Skelter" was written, albeit misspelled, in blood on a wall at the Tate murder. A decade later, John Lennon was shot and killed across the street from the Dakota, where *Rosemary's Baby* had been filmed.

This House Is Clean

1982's *Poltergeist* tells the story of a family tormented by vengeful spirits, because their new house was built over a graveyard with the bodies left in the ground. When it came time for the prop department to source skeletons for the infamous scene with JoBeth Williams in the muddy pool, contrary to what one might expect, it was cheaper to buy real human skeletons than realistic plastic ones. (They only told Williams about that afterwards.) In a case of "life imitating art," specifically in regard to disrespectful treatment of dead bodies, the cast seemed to be plagued by bad fortune. The curse extended not only the original film, but to its sequels as well. Shortly after *Poltergeist* was released, Dominique Dunne, who played the older sister, was strangled to death by her abusive ex-boyfriend, ending her career before it began. Heather O'Rourke, the adorable blonde girl who uttered the iconic line "They're heeere," died during bowel obstruction surgery after suffering cardiac arrest and septic shock due to being misdiagnosed by her doctor. She was only twelve years old. Julian Beck of *Poltergeist II: The Other Side* died of stomach cancer before the film was released. Will Sampson, also known for playing Chief in *One Flew Over the Cuckoo's Nest*, died the following year from complications of a heart-lung transplant.

Genghis Khan't

Choosing the right location to shoot a film is a pivotal decision. You have to consider things like lighting conditions, availability of utilities, and proximity to noise sources such as airports. What you should not have to consider is the radiation level, but you should not ignore it either. The producers of the 1956 movie *The Conqueror* chose an area of Utah desert a hundred miles away from the Nevada nuclear test site. They also chose to cast John Wayne as Genghis Khan, if that helps to establish the caliber of decision-making in play. Throughout the 1950s, around a hundred nuclear bombs of varying intensities were detonated at the Nevada test site. The mushroom clouds could reach tens of thousands of feet high; desert winds would carry radioactive particles all the way to Utah. The area in which *The Conqueror* filmed was likely blanketed in this dust.

The Conqueror, costarring Susan Hayward, Agnes Moorehead, and Pedro Armendáriz, was a moderate box office success but a critical failure, and soon found itself on "worst films of all time" lists. The true legacy of the film had yet to be revealed. Of the 220 people who worked on the production, 92 developed some form of cancer, with 46 dying of it, including Moorehead and Armendáriz. The director, Dick Powell, died of lymphoma in 1963. Wayne developed lung cancer and then the stomach cancer that would kill him in 1979. Wayne would remain convinced that his chain-smoking was to blame for the cancers, even as friends tried to convince him it was from exposure to radiation. Wayne's sons, who visited the set during filming and actually played with Geiger counters among the contaminated rocks, both developed tumors. Susan Hayward died from brain cancer in 1975 at fifty-seven.

The authorities had declared the area to be safe from radioactive fallout in 1954, even though abnormal levels of radiation were detected. Modern research has shown that the soil in some areas near the filming site would have remained radioactive for sixty years. Howard Hughes, the producer of *The Conqueror*, came to realize in the early 1970s that people who were involved with the production were dying. As the person who approved the filming location, Hughes felt culpable and paid twelve million to buy all existing copies of the film. Though the link between the location and the cancers that cannot be definitely proven, experts argue that the preponderance of cases goes well beyond coincidence.

Speed Kills, Repeatedly

James Dean was on the cusp of stardom when he died in a car crash before the release of *Rebel without a Cause*. A second or two before his Porsche 550 Spyder, nicknamed "Little Bastard," crashed into a more substantial Ford sedan, Dean, according to his mechanic who was a passenger in the car, said "That guy's gotta stop...he'll see us." He did not. The tragedy did not end with the crash. Many people believe that Porsche to be irrefutably cursed. The wrecked carcass of Little Bastard was sold at auction for $2,500 ($24,000 today) and soon after it slipped off its trailer and broke a mechanic's leg. The engine and drivetrain were sold to two different buyers, who later raced each other in cars containing the parts. One lost control and hit a tree, killing him instantly; the other was seriously injured when his brakes suddenly locked up and his car rolled over while going into a turn. Two tires from the Porsche that were undamaged in Dean's accident were sold, only to simultaneously blow out and cause the new owner's car to run off the road. The remains of the Porsche caught the attention of two would-be thieves. One severely lacerated an arm trying to steal the steering wheel and the other was injured trying to remove the bloodstained seat. Due to all these strange and disturbing incidents, the owner donated Little Bastard to a highway safety exhibit. The garage that housed the exhibit caught fire and burned to the ground, but the cursed car was virtually undamaged.

Dean was not the only cast member from *Rebel without a Cause* to die unexpectedly. Sal Mineo was stabbed to death outside his apartment, and Natalie Wood drowned under questionable circumstances.

Pre-production Hell

Some films are so jinxed, they can't even get to filming. A bestselling book should make for a successful movie, provided your lead actor does not die. Repeatedly. *A Confederacy of Dunces* may have come under an ominous cloud because it was published after the suicide of author John Kennedy Toole. *A Confederacy of Dunces* tells the story of Ignatius J. Reilly, a lazy man looking for work while living with his mother in New Orleans. When Hollywood came calling, it set off a chain of tragedies and failures. The first person cast in the lead, John Belushi, died of a drug overdose in 1982 before filming began. The next production was to be directed by John Waters, but his chosen lead (and the inspiration for Ursula in Disney's *The Little Mermaid*), drag queen Divine, died of a heart attack in 1988. The same fate befell John Candy after the role passed to him in 1997. Next was Chris Farley, who died of a drug overdose later that year. The curse did not limit itself to lead actors. The head of the Film Commission of Louisiana was murdered, and the entire city of New Orleans was nearly wiped out by Hurricane Katrina. Despite all that, producers continued to try to make the movie. Versions starring John Goodman, Will Ferrell, and Zach Galifianakis were all announced, and all faded away un-filmed, though fortunately all three actors are alive as of this publication. Filmmaker Steven Soderbergh was quoted as saying, "I think it's cursed. I'm not prone to superstition, but that project has got bad mojo on it."

Mordecai Richler's 1963 novel *The Incomparable Atuk* is a fish-out-of-water story about an Inuit man who moves to New York City. John Belushi read for the role of Atuk before his death. In 1988, production began with shock comic Sam Kinison in the lead. Eight days in, Kinison demanded script rewrites, becoming so difficult that his manager dropped him and United Artists studio sued him. Production never resumed, and Kinison would be killed in a head-on collision a few years later. The role then went to John Candy; see above. The curse of *Atuk* also claimed some collateral damage in the form of screenwriter Michael O'Donoghue, who read the script with Candy and died of a sudden brain hemorrhage later that year. Again, Chris Farley was chosen after Candy's death. Farley knew about the apparent curse but said he did not care. He did not live to play the role. Farley's *Saturday Night Live* costar Phil Hartman was said to be up for a supporting role, but was tragically killed by his wife in a murder-suicide.

CHAPTER 5

Business & Technology

FAKE A NEED AND FILL IT

"Unethical advertising uses falsehoods to deceive the public.
Ethical advertising uses the truth to deceive the public."[2]

—**Vilhjalmur Stefansson**

The Patriarch of PR

The classic American breakfast of bacon, eggs, and toast falls somewhere between the bread-and-fruit-based Continental breakfast and the "how many kinds of sausage can fit on one plate?" approach of the "full English" breakfast. As classic as it may seem, bacon has only been on the breakfast table for about a century. Before that, the average American would probably have started their day with bread or porridge made of whatever grain was prevalent in their region and a cup of tea or coffee. Packaged cereal dealt meat another blow as it proliferated after the industrial revolution. The resurgent popularity of the processed pork belly can be attributed to one man, the pioneer of public relations, Edward Bernays.

Bernays started life in Austria with a leg-up on publicity by virtue of being Sigmund Freud's nephew. Bernays studied the work of his uncle and others to develop theories on human behavior, especially the behavior of people in groups. If his accomplishments are anything to go by, his theories hold water. He convinced the public that water fluoridation was safe; the glass in their bathroom was full of scary germs, so they should use disposable Dixie Cups; pocket watches were too cumbersome and wristwatches were not just for ladies; and President Coolidge should be reelected. He described his techniques with the phrase "the engineering of consent." Bernays also organized the CIA's overthrow of the socialist government of Guatemala on behalf of United Fruit Company, which is Chiquita today, but that's a story for another time.

---

2   Does this quote come to us from a real-life Don Draper or from a Ralph Nader-like consumer guardian? Nope. Vilhjalmur Stefansson was a Canadian-born Icelandic-American Arctic explorer and ethnologist (1879–1962).

In the 1920s, Bernays was approached by the Beech-Nut Packing Company, producers of everything from pork, coffee, baby food, and gum. Beech-Nut needed to sell more bacon, but there was insufficient demand. Bernays consulted Beech-Nut's staff doctor, who suggested that a heavier breakfast would be healthier "because the body loses energy during the night and needs it during the day." Bernays then surveyed 4,500 doctors, asking them which would be a healthier breakfast for a person who needs energy for their day, a light grain-based breakfast or a heavier meat-and-egg-based breakfast. Most doctors chose the bacon and eggs. This "study" was published in major newspapers and magazines across the country. Bacon sales, and Beech-Nut's profits, rose significantly. This was, of course, decades before we understood the dangers of saturated fat and nitrates.

It doesn't get more American than this...thanks to Edward Bernays.

Bernays is also to credit, or blame, with the widespread adoption of another bad habit—smoking, specifically by women. After soldiers returned home from WWI, tobacco use soared, since cigarettes had been included in the soldiers' rations. It became a symbol of manly pride and even patriotism. For women, on the other hand, smoking guaranteed they would become social pariahs, since only "fallen women" smoked. If a woman in a movie was smoking, she was a vamp, a character without morals. A short-lived ordinance was even passed in New York that landed at least one woman in jail for lighting up. When women did smoke, they did so in private.

WWI had seen women gain more independence and a smidgen of gender equality after the war effort brought them jobs outside the home. George Washington Hill, president of American Tobacco Company, which manufactured Lucky Strike cigarettes, wanted to capitalize on this. He hired Bernays to make smoking appealing to women, despite the stigma. Bernays consulted with psychoanalyst A. A. Brill, who offered the Freudian theory that it was normal for women to smoke because of oral fixation. Brill stated, "Today, the emancipation of women has suppressed many of their feminine desires. More women now do the same work as men do. Many women bear no children; those who do bear have fewer children. Feminine traits are masked. Cigarettes, which are equated with men, become torches of freedom."

To display these "torches of freedom," Bernays assembled a group of carefully selected women. They had to be respectable and attractive, but not so attractive that they would look like paid models or worse, loose women. The first of Bernay's ladies to hit the streets was Bertha Hunt, Bernays' own secretary. On Easter Sunday 1929, at the height of Easter parade, Hunt stepped out onto the crowded 5th Avenue and began smoking a Lucky Strike. As she walked, Hunt told the *New York Times* that she got the idea to smoke in public so brazenly after a man asked her to put out her cigarette because it embarrassed him. "I talked it over with my friends, and we decided it was high time something was done about the situation." Ten young women followed her, brandishing their own "torches." The *New York Times* ran a story the next day entitled, "Group of Girls Puff at Cigarettes as a Gesture of Freedom." The sensation was immediate. Papers across the country carried the picture. How did word get around so quickly of such a small happening? The press had been notified in advance by Bernays' agency.

The walk was seen as a protest for equality, a sufficient camouflage to keep Bernays, Brill, and American Tobacco hidden. The rates of women smoking rose from 12 percent in 1929 to 18 percent in 1935, peaking at 33 percent in 1965. Bernays was also behind campaign that pushed cigarettes as a diet aid with the famous slogan, "Reach for a Lucky instead of a sweet." For convincing women to take up an expensive and deadly habit, Bernays' "thirty pieces of silver" equates to over $620,000.

> Though Marlboro cigarettes are irrevocably tied to the macho Marlboro Man, they were originally marketed to women with the tagline, "Mild as May."

Hair Today, Gone Tomorrow

The women who smoked in the Easter parade wore the fashion of the day, namely sleeveless dresses, garments that both liberated them from modest Victorian-style gowns and made them slaves to the razor. A typical Victorian dress covered the wearer from neck to toes, with sleeves down to the wrist. Body hair was one's own business, because no one else could see it. The sleeveless flapper dress exposed underarm hair. That was not a problem since everyone had armpit hair, after all. Gillette wanted women to think it was a problem.

The safety razor, invented in 1901, had made Gillette a household name, thanks in no small part to a contract with the US Army to supply every soldier with a razor. However, only men were buying. Half of the population did not touch the product. Gillette's approach was to make women embarrassed about their default down. They dubbed the razor the Milady Décolleté Gillette and advertised it in 1917, with lines like: "...one that solves an embarrassing personal problem. Milady Décolleté Gillette is welcomed by women everywhere—now that a feature of good dressing and good grooming is to keep the underarm white and smooth." Their goal was to leave each reader feeling that if she did not shave her armpits, she would be the only one walking around so unfashionable. Gillette sought to make shaving sound like an intrinsic part of womanhood, as if it had always been there. Hair removal for either or both genders has been common around the world and across time, but not for American women then. Gillette referred to the activity as "smoothing" rather than "shaving," because shaving was what men did. Their ads even forwent words like "razor" and "blade."

At first, the armpits were the only problem area. Leg hair would get its vilification in the 1920s, when hemlines went higher. Gillette had a hurdle to overcome—the increasingly popular stocking. Stockings were a faster, easier, and less-bloody way to hide leg hair. It would take the pin-up style of the 1940s to take stockings out of the running. The iconic picture of Betty Grable in her white bathing suit with her "million-dollar legs" set the beauty standard and women were told that it was their patriotic duty during WWII to be pretty, to "Keep up morale for national defense." The war also meant that fewer women wore stockings because nylon was needed for the war effort. Many women would darken their legs with makeup, tinted lotion, or even coffee to give the appearance of stockings, sometimes drawing a "seam" up the back of their legs with eyeliner. That would not work if they had hair on their legs, so shaving became the necessity that razor manufacturers had claimed it was. Those women taught the habit to their daughters, the generation of the mini skirt, who taught it to their daughters. Depilated legs and underarms are now an ingrained social construct and a multi-billion-dollar industry.

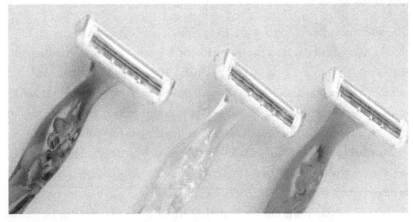

Don't forget to be ashamed of your body hair!

Breathe into Your Hand

Like being seen with unshaven legs, another social faux pas people were taught to fear was having bad breath. Not simply bad breath, but a scary-sounding condition called halitosis. Of course, the bacterial playground that is the human mouth has been prone to olfactory offenses for millennia, and people have had plants, potions, and pastilles to combat it for almost as long. However, it took a company with a "cure" to convince people that they had a serious health issue.

In the 1860s, Dr. Joseph Lister was an early crusader for germ theory and sanitary medical conditions at a time when a doctor would wear the same blood-soaked apron for hours and would be offended if you suggested that he wash his hands. With antiseptics like carbolic acid and phenol, Lister was able to reduce the mortality rate for amputees in his ward from 45–50 percent to 15 percent. This was also the age of patent medicines, when you could bottle any syrup or pill and claim it cured every disease and condition known to man. Inspired by Lister, Dr. Joseph Lawrence and Dr. Jordan Lambert created a phenol-based surgical disinfectant and dubbed it Listerine. It did not sell well, so they tried marketing it as a floor cleaner, dandruff treatment, hair tonic, deodorant, and as a "beneficial remedy" for diphtheria, dysentery, gonorrhea, and even smallpox.

Listerine was advertised to women as a vaginal douche. As horrific as that sounds, it was probably better than some of the other products being marketed for that purpose, including Lysol.

It would not be until years later, when the company was run by Lambert's son, Gerard, that the product finally found its niche as a mouthwash. To boost sales, Gerard devised to turn bad breath from a minor nuisance to a medical condition, and an embarrassing one at that. He combined the Latin word for breath, *halitus*, and the Greek suffix *-osis*, meaning a medical condition, to invent the word "halitosis." Halitosis lent Listerine the authoritative air it needed for a fantastically successful advertising campaign, creating a market for the novel product of mouthwash. Ads were run with either old ad copy or the new halitosis angle, using coupons to track how people responded to each version. Four times as many halitosis coupons were redeemed. Listerine focused its efforts on creating the fear of halitosis, and sales rose by a third in the first month. From then on, they took out a procession of ads suggesting that the reader has bad breath, but their friends and family were too polite to tell them, that bad breath was holding them back, and they did not even know it. Of course, Listerine, and only Listerine, could fix it. One of the most popular ads featured a forlorn woman and the phrase, "always a bridesmaid, never a bride," which Listerine is credited with adding to the common parlance. To this day, in marketing, creating a fear so you can sell people the solution is called "the halitosis appeal."

Did You Load It?

Though it would be more than a century before the pound sign became a hashtag, you could sum up the invention of the automatic dishwasher as #richpeopleproblems. Wealthy socialite, Josephine Cochrane, the wife of a politician in the 1880s, was tired of her kitchen staff breaking china dishes and glasses after every party she threw. They were expensive and took months to replace by mail-order. With no other apparent concerns in her day-to-day life, it was enough to drive Cochrane into the woodshed next to her home in search of a solution. She measured her plates, bowls, and glasses, and created wire compartments to fit. These compartments were secured around a wheel in a copper boiler. A motor turned the dishes, and hot, soapy water squirted up at them. The "Cochrane dishwasher" so impressed the inventor's friends that they wanted to order them for their own "clumsy" kitchen help.

News of the invention spread to hotels and restaurants, where the breakage associated with their high-volume dishwashing was a costly concern. It was clear to Cochrane that there was a market for her product, so she patented the design and started a company that would eventually become KitchenAid. Her design even won an award at the 1893 Chicago World's Fair for "best mechanical construction, durability, and adaptation to its line of work." While restaurants and hotels eagerly purchased the original large-capacity machine, there was initially nothing for the home market. In 1914, the company offered for sale, for the first time in history, an automatic device to clean a family's dishes. However, the response from the buying public was less enthusiastic than the company was hoping for.

There were a few reasons housewives were not clamoring for the new device. Even if a family had a water heater capable of reaching the temperature the dishwasher needed to do its job properly, the dishwasher required more water than many hot water heaters of the time held. Water softeners would not be invented for another decade, and the "hard," mineralized water in many parts of the country kept the soap from lathering enough to spray-clean the dishes. There was also a more human factor. Cochrane assumed the average housewife would give anything to be relieved of the drudgery of dishwashing. This was a guess on her part, as Cochrane had never washed a sink of dishes in her privileged life. However, when housewives were surveyed, the company found that, of all the laborious tasks set before them each day, they minded dishwashing the least. Many reported that it was actually their quiet time at the end of the day. (One shudders to think.)

The company tried a different tactic, claiming that their dishwasher used water at a higher temperature than human hands could bear, so dishes were not only cleaner, but more sanitary. This did not work, either. The home dishwasher remained a novelty until the post-war economic boom of the 1950s, when convenience became a key marketing angle.

VETERAN OF THE FORMAT WARS

Coke or Pepsi? New York or LA? Cats or dogs? iPod or Zune? That last one is easy. The competition between two titans of technology to be *the* music player could have raged for years. Instead, Microsoft's Zune never achieved more than 10 percent of the market, taking two years to sell as many units as Apple sold in a month. A few years later, Zune was quietly shuffled off to the format graveyard.

Let the Record Show...

For as long as we have had media on which to record, there have been competing formats, going all the way back to early phonographs. The first format war was between Thomas Edison and Emile Berliner. Edison created the wax cylinder in the 1880s as a means of recording telephone conversations, but they soon became a popular format for music. In the following decade, Berliner released the familiar disk record. Disk records were originally used in children's toys, and their sound quality was terrible. After several modifications, disk records were able to rival Edison's cylinders in sound quality, sparking a battle that lasted nearly twenty years. Despite the cylinder's initial dominance, disk records won. By the late 1920s, Edison had started marketing disk records of his own. The main deciding factor was the production process. Disk records were cheaper and easier to make, since they could simply be stamped on a press. Once they started being recorded on both sides, people were able to get twice as much music for the same price. Disk records were also easier to ship and could be stored on a shelf like books.

Record design continued to change over the decades before cassette tapes were popularized. There was the Edison diamond disc, which used "hills and dales" instead of grooves; the tone needle from a standard record player would ruin them. There were 16 ⅔ RPM records, half the speed of the 33 ⅓ RPM record that were standard for recorded music. Only at the height of their availability could you even buy a record player with a 16-⅔ RPM speed setting.

> 16 ⅔ RPM records were too slow for high fidelity sound, so they were used mostly for spoken word. They became the first "talking books" for the blind.

Disco on the Go

When 8-track tapes hit the shelves in the 1960s, they were a revolution. No longer subject to the whims of radio, you could listen to the songs you wanted in your car or out-and-about with a boombox. Developed by jet designer William Lear, the 8-track cartridge contained ¼-inch tape running in a continuous loop around a hub. The tape was divided lengthwise into eight channels or tracks. The tape head played two tracks at a time to achieve stereo. A metal strip connected the ends of the tape. When the strip connected with a solenoid in the player, the playback head shifting across the tape to continue playing, causing the trademark clunk sound. If nothing broke, an 8-track would theoretically play forever. The format got a boost in 1967, when Ford made 8-track players optional equipment on all their cars.

8-tracks were the way of the future, for about a decade. By the time the neon '80s dawned, 8-tracks had been relegated to trash bins and garage sales. The layout of songs on the original album might not line up with the tracks on the tape, so it was common for the music to fade out and back in during a song as it transitioned to a new track. The 8-tracks could not rewind, so if you missed your favorite part, you had to wait for the song to come around again. There was also a phenomenon called bleed-through. If the playback heads became misaligned even slightly, one track would play faintly in the background of another track. Less damning, but still a black mark, was the album art; they were just stickers that cracked, faded, and peeled. The primary reason the 8-track went extinct was because it was patently unreliable. The cartridge itself was hard-wearing and heat-resistant, but the internal components could fail at any moment. Where vinyl and other formats have maintained a hard-core following, no one is really fighting to bring back 8-tracks.

The first karaoke machine was an 8-track player. In 1971, Daisuke Inoue combined a microphone, amplifier, coin box, and 8-track tape player, which he called the 8-Juke and, sadly, never patented.

Home Movies

Readers of a certain age will remember TV commercials for home movies that ended with two different prices, one for VHS and one for Betamax. In the early 1980s, two companies fought a pitched battle for home video dominance—Sony with its Betamax format and JVC with VHS. Spoiler alert: VHS won. The Betamax video cassette recorder was the first on the market in the US by nearly two years. Released in 1975, it weighed a monstrous thirty-six pounds (or sixteen kilograms) and cost the equivalent of six thousand dollars. Blank cassettes were about seventy dollars in today's money. Recording television shows was a revolutionary concept, and the entertainment industry felt threatened. Universal Studios and Walt Disney Productions filed a lawsuit in 1976 to halt the sale of the Betamax, claiming that film and TV producers would lose millions to unauthorized duplication and distribution. They made it all the way to the Supreme Court, where five justices voted to allow home recording. (This was the case that Mr. Rogers testified in, on behalf of children who were in school when his show aired.)

"We Are the Champions" plays in the background.

Both Betamax and VHS VCRs solved the same problem—storing information compactly on a magnetic tape. The machine pulled the tape forward to a spinning silver drum. The drum had two electromagnets, called heads, on opposite sides that read the information on the tape. That rotating head allowed for a more compact recorder. In previous attempts at the VCR, the tape moved rather than the heads, which meant you needed a lot of tape. It took a seven inch (or twenty-eight centimeter) reel to record one hour; a movie would need a cassette more than a foot wide. Rotating heads made home VCRs feasible.

Betamax was the superior format, with better-constructed machines, higher resolution, superior sound, and a more stable image. So why did Betamax lose? The VHS VCR was five pounds (or two kilograms) lighter, which makes a huge difference in mass production, impacting material costs, assembly time, shipping costs, etc. The earliest Betamax tapes only played for one hour, while VHS tapes played for two hours, long enough for a movie.

The death blow for Betamax was the rental market. While Betamax poured its corporate energy into ads declaring, "Watch whatever, whenever," JVC created relationships with the budding video rental industry. As this market grew, VHS dominated in titles. Retailers began giving more shelf space to the slightly more dominant brand, which then dominated even more. Betamax limped along a lot longer than you might think—production of Betamax recorders continued until 2002. The last tapes rolled off the production line in 2016, the same year the last VCR was manufactured.

"Frickin' Laser Beams"

There was a third horse in the home video race—Laserdisc. Magnavox trotted out their own in-home entertainment system in 1978 called "DiscoVision," which encoded analog data onto a disc read by a laser. This new technology had dramatically better picture and audio quality than magnetic tape. It was also capable of storing multiple audio tracks, allowing for things like director's commentary to be added. DiscoVision players cost about $2,300 today, but they still sold out quickly in the test market of Atlanta. The soon-to-be-genericized name "Laserdisc" came from Pioneer when they offered their own player a few years later. Pioneer got their price down to the equivalent of $1,500, and with celebrities like Ray Charles and Mr. Wizard (Bill Nye for us old folks) pitching the product, Laserdisc was on the upswing.

As with Betamax, cost put the kibosh on Laserdisc. The Laserdisc player was technologically complex and bulky, making it expensive to manufacture and ship. Storage was also an issue. The Laserdisc stored the video and audio in analog form, rather than digitally like a DVD, and that lack of compression, combined with a large frame rate, resulted in early discs only being able to store thirty minutes of video per side. Later models barely managed to double that. This meant that, like a record, you had to get up frequently to turn the disc over or swap it out for the next one, after which it would take thirty seconds for the half pound disc to spin back up to full speed. While Laserdiscs were theoretically cheaper to make, the sheer volume of cassettes being sold brought their price to manufacture down to a dollar apiece by the end of the 1980s, while a Laserdisc cost five dollars. A new release movie on Laserdisc would cost seventy to eighty dollars today; the same movie on VHS was half that. Another significant advantage of VHS was the ability to record, which was possible with Laserdisc, but not practical. VHS tape were also more durable—the slightest scratch meant death to a Laserdisc. Poor manufacturing quality of early discs meant that they were also susceptible to "disc rot," oxidation of the reflective layer of the disc that resulted in blobs or constellations of discoloration. (This can happen with DVDs and CDs, too, if they are stored flat instead of upright.) Laserdisc did find staying power in situations where a program might be watched again and again, such as in schools, because they did not degrade with use like magnetic tape.

The Sorry State of Sony

The Sony Corporation seemed to have more than their share of failed formats. In the mid-1980s, Sony introduced the Digital Audio Tape as a successor to the analog cassette tape for consumers, combining the spinning-head technology from VCRs with digital encoding. For a time, they were the standard audio format for situations like bands submitting demo tapes to record labels. DATs were controversial, with the Recording Industry Association of America lobbying to prevent DAT machines being sold in the US for fear of high-quality album copying. Though they were the top choice for musicians looking for a recording contract, DATs never really caught on with consumers, thanks in part to their expensive players. Sony officially killed the DAT format in 2005, by then, it had been overtaken by recordable CDs, without having ever lived up to the success of cassettes.

1993 saw the launch of two soon-to-fail products: MiniDisc and ATRAC Audio Compression. MiniDisc seemed to solve the issues inherent in both cassettes and CDs. Unlike cassettes, the quality was crystal clear. It would not warp in the heat, skip when bumped, or be damaged by its player; and the quality did not degrade with use. Though MiniDisc could have been successful, Sony added stern digital copy protection, which, combined with high media prices, and the steep cost of buying a player/recorder, meant it never took off. ATRAC was a proprietary file type for the MiniDisc, and later the solid-state Walkman. In 1998, Sony developed the MemoryStick, which could only be used with their digital cameras and music players. If you wanted to buy a Sony camera, you had to spend more money on their specific file storage media for it. Though some devices still use it, Sony had to concede to the rocketing popularity of SD cards and eventually began supporting them. Proprietary loses to open standard again.

A MiniDisk player.

In 2005, Sony put some of its MiniDisc thinking into the engineering and design of the Universal Media Disc for movies and games on the PlayStation Portable. The size of the media had a direct effect on the design of the PlayStation Portable, making it bulkier than it otherwise would have been. UMDs never saw widespread support from movie studios, and production of UMD movies was significantly cut back the following year. The successor console, the PSP Go, ditched the UMD in favor of digital downloads.

While the echoes of the great Beta vs. VHS battle still resonated, a new home video format war was about to kick off—Blu-ray vs. HD-DVD. Sony came armed with Blu-ray, and Toshiba had HD-DVD, with the PlayStation 3 and Xbox 360 ready to serve as Trojan horses. Like Betamax, Toshiba's HD-DVD had a viewing experience at least as good as its competitor and was the first to launch. It was also the first to fail. Sony promised its Blu-ray format could handle higher capacity and even interactivity, while Toshiba claimed HD-DVD would make up for lower capacity in other areas, like being cheaper and easier to manufacture at factories that were already making DVDs. As for content, major studio support weighed heavily in Blu-ray's favor. Once

Warner Bros. withdrew their support for HD-DVD on the eve of the 2008 Consumer Electronics Show, the war was over; Toshiba conceded a month later. Sony had successfully pushed Blu-ray into millions of homes with its PS3, even though the PS3 initially trailed the Xbox 360 and Nintendo Wii in sales.

In-Flex-ible

There was another format that could not compete, but deserves to be in this gallery of failures—Flexplay or EZ-D. Do you like renting movies, but hate returning them? Do you enjoy having a limited time to watch movies and being left with a bunch of unplayable garbage discs in your house? Like the failed DIVX before it, Flexplay discs would turn black and become unreadable after forty-eight hours At least Flexplay had the sense to work in standard players, rather than requiring its own machine that had to be hooked up to a phone line to communicate with a main server, as DIVX had. (DIVX was created by Circuit City, one of many decisions that precipitated their demise.) Neither DIVX nor Flexplay discs had any special features, just the movie. The technology was originally intended as an alternative means for the short-term rental of newly released movies. For those too young to remember, you were only allowed to rent new release movies for two days. Except, these were not new releases. For fear of Flexplay taking revenue away from DVDs, the movies released on Flexplay were at least two months old, by which time most people who wanted to see the movie already had. The forty-eight-hour countdown did not start the first time you pressed play, but when you opened it. Flexplay discs were shipped in a vacuum-sealed packaging. A clear dye inside the disc would react with oxygen once the package was opened, and then turn black over about forty-eight hours, rendering the disc unplayable. If unopened, the shelf life of the sealed package was said to be "about a year." The manufacturer claimed the discs were recyclable, but environmental groups condemned them for making a disposable version of a durable product. You also had to take it back to the store for recycling, thus negating the whole system. The brand limped along for a few years, being bought and sold by different companies, like Disney, then HowStuffWorks, and finally Staples, who sold them at the rock bottom clearance price of ninety-nine cents each less than a year later.

LAWS OF THE INTERNET

The internet may be on the cutting edge of technology, but the humans who inhabit it make it seem more like the Wild Wild West—an anarchic place full of ruffians, hooligans, and ne'er-do-wells. The internet actually has a variety of laws, though they are not enforced by a central authority, like civic law, or naturally occurring, like the law of gravity. The laws of the internet are more like axioms or postulates, summations of behavior that can be dropped into a discussion thread to make one's point. Many of these laws date back to Usenet, a cross between a discussion board and a file-sharing service that was effectively the first social network back in the days of dial-up modems.

Poe's Law

> "Without a winking smiley or other blatant display of humor, it is utterly impossible to parody a Creationist in such a way that someone won't mistake for the genuine article."

The original conversation in which Poe's Law was put forth was about creationism, but it has since been expanded to apply to any extreme or inflexible belief, or any point of view at all. While the internet facilitates communication around the world at lightning speed, it has considerable difficulty conveying tone. Sincerity can be mistaken for sarcasm and facetious comments can be taken for fanaticism. For example, if you were to read the transcript of a Stephen Colbert monologues from *The Colbert Report* without context or the benefit of hearing Colbert's inflection, the character would seem like a far-right extremist with a transient grasp on reality. However, the insertion of a few crying-with-laughter emojis would help to establish the mocking nature of the content. "When social networks used to be bounded by interests, the joke teller could expect that their audience was in on the joke," says Whitney Phillips, author of *This Is Why We Can't Have Nice Things: Mapping the Relationship Between Online Trolling and Internet Culture.* "Now a single re-tweet can cause spontaneous global amplification." The statement is then floating around entirely context-free.

Poe's Law goes beyond tonal misunderstandings when internet trolls get involved. A troll is a person who creates havoc, starts arguments, and generally make the internet less pleasant and more difficult to use for everyone else. Poe's Law has become an escape hatch for such people. On the rare occasion that a troll is taken to task for their behavior, they can invoke Poe's Law as a shield to declare that "it was just a joke," and everyone else was too dumb to get it. Trolls also use it to spread disinformation, the more mischievous, the better. The denizens of the forum site 4chan.com has excelled at this with a fake propaganda campaign that included, among other things, that the "OK" hand gesture (thumb and forefinger circle) was the white supremacist version of a gang sign. When that "news" got beyond the boundaries of 4chan.com, it was mistaken for trustworthy information and spread. When self-described "national security reporter" Mike Cernovich posted a photo of himself and colleague Cassandra Fairbanks doing the gesture, *Fusion* journalist Emma Roller re-tweeted it with the message, "just two people doing a white power hand gesture in the White House." Roller then found herself on the receiving end of a defamation lawsuit. It would be dismissed because, ignorance notwithstanding, the plaintiffs could not prove that Roller's statement was made from malice.

Cunningham's Law

> "The best way to get the right answer on the internet is not to ask a question, it's to post the wrong answer."

If anyone is worthy of being the namesake to a rule about how information is added to the internet, it would be Ward Cunningham, the programmer who developed the first wiki, or user-built knowledge base. (Cunningham did not create Wikipedia, but he did create the software that Wikipedia originally used.) Like the other internet laws, it's based in human behavior, specifically in people's innate desire to be right. Answering a question posted online smacks of effort with limited satisfaction. Correcting someone else's statement pays dividends in a sense of superiority.

"Cunningham's Law" was coined in 2010 in a comment on a *New York Times* article left by Inel executive Steven McGeady. The article called for readers to suggest "novel eponymous laws" to add to the likes of Murphy's Law ("Anything that can go wrong, will"). According to McGeady, Cunningham's Law was "named after Ward Cunningham, a colleague of mine at Tektronix. This was his advice to me in the early 1980s." In the early 1980s, the electronic bulletin boards were not even called the Usenet yet, and the web as we know it was technologically impossible. The law is much more timeless than its name. Even Arthur Conan Doyle mentioned this human tendency through his character Sherlock Holmes, "People don't like you telling them things. They love to contradict you."

Godwin's Law (or Godwin's Rule of Hitler Analogies)

"As an online discussion grows longer, the probability of a comparison involving Nazis or Hitler approaches 1."

Godwin's Law was the decree of American attorney Mike Godwin, who worked with the Electronic Frontier Foundation and was the author of *Cyber Rights: Defending Free Speech in the Digital Age*. Regardless of the topic or scope of an online discussion, if it goes on long enough, someone will eventually compare someone or something to Adolf Hitler or his actions—*reductio ad Hitlerum*. At that point, the thread loses any chance of a productive outcome.

Godwin described his law as an experiment in memetics, the study of the spread and evolution of information. "Although deliberately framed as if it were a law of nature or of mathematics," Godwin wrote, "its purpose has always been rhetorical and pedagogical: I wanted folks who glibly compared someone else to Hitler to think a bit harder about the Holocaust." Godwin's Law isn't only what happens when the mention of Nazis ends a conversation, but it's proactively used by some to forcibly end discussions. With that in mind, a Facebook user reached out to Godwin, asking him to make a public statement after the August 2017 "Unite the Right" march in Charlottesville, Virginia. "By all means," he responded, "compare these s***heads to Nazis. Again and again."

Brandolini's Bulls*** Asymmetry Principle

> "The amount of energy needed to refute bulls*** is an order of magnitude [i.e. ten times] bigger than to produce it."

Alberto Brandolini, an Italian software engineer and author, put his eponymous law forward during the XP2014 technology conference, after watching a journalist and politician arguing on a talk show. It's important to know that this principle does not apply to mistakes or inaccuracies, but to a specific form of misinformation. In his essay "On Bulls***," Harry Frankfurt of the Philosophy Faculty at Princeton University characterized a liar as one who knows and cares about the truth but deliberately sets out to mislead, while the "bulls***ter" does not care about the truth one way or the other.

"It is impossible for someone to lie unless he thinks he knows the truth. Producing bulls*** requires no such conviction.... When an honest man speaks, he says only what he believes to be true; and for the liar, it is correspondingly indispensable that he considers his statements to be false. For the bulls***ter, however, all these bets are off: he is neither on the side of the true nor on the side of the false.... He does not care whether the things he says describe reality correctly. He just picks them out, or makes them up, to suit his purpose."

See also the Yiddish proverb, "a stone thrown into the well by a fool cannot be retrieved by fifty wise men."

McKean/Skitt/Hartman's Law

> "Any article or statement about correct grammar, punctuation, or spelling is bound to contain at least one error."

On his blog *Words & Stuff*, author and editor Jed Hartman asserted Hartman's Law of Prescriptivist Retaliation on the ironic but inevitable inclusion of errors when correcting someone else's error. Prescriptivism, or language purism, is the viewpoint that one way of speaking or writing is superior to others and should be held as the standard. Hartman was far from the only person to notice this phenomenon. Erin McKean, editor of *Verbatim* and self-declared "Dictionary Evangelist" coined McKean's Law: "Any correction of the speech or writing of others will contain at least one grammatical, spelling, or typographical error." Likewise, a member of an English grammar Usenet, Bryan Lord (username Skitt) issued Skitt's Law: "The likelihood of an error in a post is directly proportional to the embarrassment it will cause the poster." He took things a step further than the other law-creators: "The effect is, of course, magnified a hundredfold if the post is in reply to Skitt himself."

Even the most skilled grammarian can fall victim to this law. Web developer, blogger, and language enthusiast Paulo Ordoveza proposed a March to End "Beg the Question" Abuse:

"For too long, we linguistic pedants have cringed, watching this phrase used, misused, and abused, again, and again, and again. 'This begs the question...' we read in the editorials, see on TV, hear on the radio, (perhaps even read in one of those newfangled 'web blogs') and we must brace ourselves as the *ignoramii* of modern society literally ask a question after the phrase."

The trouble here is, the plural of "ignoramus" is not "ignoramii." "Ignoramus" is not a noun, but the present indicative of the verb "ignoro," meaning "we do not know." After being borrowed into English, its plural was simply "ignoramuses." Even if "ignoramus" were a noun, the plural would be "ignorami" or "ignoramūs." However, it's worth pointing out that Ordoveza's article was published on April 1, i.e. April Fool's Day, to wit his "mistake" was probably intentional. Not sure if the author was joking or not? That's Poe's Law in action again.

Betteridge's Law of Headlines

> "Any headline that ends in a question mark
> can be answered by the word 'no.' "

The law is named for British technology journalist Ian Betteridge, who concluded a blog post with the idea, though he did not proclaim it as a law. It has been cited by other names since 1991, including "Davis's Law," though no source has cited who the eponymous Davis was. There is a corollary in scientific circles called Hinchliffe's Rule, after physicist Ian Hinchliffe, who stated that if the title of a research paper is in the form of a yes/no question, the answer will be "no."

Lewis's Law

> "The comments on any article about
> feminism justify feminism."

British journalist and the former deputy editor of the *New Statesman*, Helen Lewis tweeted this law in 2012. It means that any pro-feminist internet content will inevitably draw misogynistic responses. As little as mentioning feminism can provoke sexist comments from three kinds of people: trolls, Incels, and men's rights activists. Trolls were covered above. "Incel" is short for "involuntary celibate," men who blame women for denying them the sex they feel entitled to. Men's rights activism began as a legitimate push for things like gender equality in child custody and better treatment of male domestic violence victims but became infested with trolls and Incels. When a feminist calls someone out for sexist remarks, they are accused of exaggerating the situation, nitpicking "normal" behavior, and/or demanding rights beyond what men have, thus proving the need for feminism.

The Law of Exclamation

> "The more exclamation points used in an email (or
> other posting), the more likely it is a complete lie.
> This is also true for excessive capital letters."

Though the concept has been acknowledged for some time, this law was codified in its present form in 2018 by Lori Robertson, managing editor of factcheck.org. The creation of the law was sparked by a wave of viral and chain-letter emails. Credible sources rarely feel compelled to use excessive punctuation, nor does it pass muster with style guides. Exclamation marks and capital letters may also be joined with deceivingly evocative (i.e., click-bait) phrases like "You won't believe…" or "…will shock you!!!" The Law of Exclamation reminds one of author Terry Pratchett's litmus test for mental stability: "Five exclamation marks, the sure sign of an insane mind."

Danth's Law

> "If you have to insist that you've won an internet argument, you've probably lost badly."

Among the benefits of arguing online rather than in person is the ability to declare oneself the supreme victor of the debate and simply close the browser. Created on the popular roleplaying game forum, RPG.net, the law is named for the permanently banned user who inspired it. A synopsis of the discussion that led to Danth's Law can be found on RPG.net:

"Having been away from his computer for a while, Danth returns to see the mockery and states that, "When this happens [people resorting to personal attacks], I usually assume that I have 'won.' Sorry if you couldn't handle my arguments."

Ten posts later, user Balthazor puts into words what is now known as "Danth's Law." Often, declaring victory is a last-ditch attempt to win by tricking people into believing that you already have. They may declare victory based purely on the amount of opposition they have faced—why would so many people dispute them if they were not the rare, clever person who actually knows better?

RPG.net also gave us Skarka's Law: "There is no subject so vile or indefensible that someone won't post positively/in defense of it."

The Streisand Effect

Attempting to suppress or remove something from the internet will make it more popular than it would have been on its own.

The turn of phrase came from Mike Masnick, founder of the Techdirt.com. In 2003, a scientific photographer took over 12,000 photos of the California coastline to document coastal erosion. Many celebrities have beachfront properties, among them singer-actress Barbra Streisand. The photos were posted online and even though the house was not identified as hers, Streisand argued that the image violated anti-paparazzi laws, demanded it be taken down, and sued for ten million dollars in damage. Before the lawsuit was filed, the image of Streisand's house had been viewed six times, two of which were by Streisand's attorneys. After the lawsuit made the news, nearly half a million people viewed the photo. The lawsuit backfired a second time when Streisand was ordered to pay $155,567 for the photographer's legal fees.

A similar situation unfolded for superstar singer Beyoncé after a Super Bowl halftime performance in 2013. BuzzFeed published an article and photo series of Beyoncé's "fiercest moments" from the show. Shortly afterward, Beyoncé's publicist contacted the website to have the most "unflattering photos" removed, with the worst one specifically listed. Like a cat sitting on a table with a glass, BuzzFeed dove directly into the bad behavior with a second article, "The Unflattering Photos Beyoncé's Publicist Doesn't Want You to See." The post included the publicist's email, and the only photos used were the "unflattering" ones. One in particular, in which Beyoncé is caught in a muscly, stiff-armed pose, with a bizarre facial expression, shot around the internet and was photoshopped to look like a weightlifter, various cartoon characters, and the Incredible Hulk.

Perhaps the most important, but least obeyed internet law is Wheaton's Law, set forth by the *Star Trek: The Next Generation* actor and first person to reach one million Twitter followers, which says simply, "Don't be a d*ck."

CHAPTER 6

Daily Life

WHAT'S A DRINK WITHOUT A NOSH?

A Night Out

Who else gets hungry when they have been drinking? Good, then around the world we go! When the superstars of beer-making tie one on, Germans enjoy *currywurst*, fried pork sausage smothered in a spiced ketchup or tomato sauce, with fries, naturally. In Thailand, the drunk food of choice is *khao phat*, fried rice with meat, egg, onions, garlic, tomatoes, and cucumber. Mexico turns to tacos, especially *barbacoa*, *lingua* (tongue), and tripe. Tripe, cow's stomach, also features in their hangover cure, a soup called *menudo*. To the north in Canada, it's *poutine*, French fries doused with gravy and cheese curds to soak up the booze. Across the pond, they go out for *kebabs*, pita stuffed with thinly sliced meat, veggies, and various sauces.

Canadian *poutine*.

Kebab refers to the meat, *shish* refers to the skewer and *doner* means it was cooked on a rotisserie.

In the Philippines, people go for *sisig*, a sweet and spicy dish made with pig's head and liver, chili peppers, and calamansi fruit. Discerning even when drunk, Italians love a fatty herbaceous pork roast sliced into pieces and stuffed between thick, buttery slices of bread. In India in general, and Mumbai specifically, the drunk food of choice is *bhurji-pav*, a spiced scrambled egg with bread. *Mandazi*, also called a Swahili coconut, is popular in Kenya and can be either savory or sweet. Sri Lanka favors *kottu*, a mixture of chopped vegetables, stir-fried egg, spices, and shredded *godamba roti* (thin, fried bread). *Jianbing*, a Chinese-style savory crepe, is not only a popular late-night snack in China, but also a breakfast food. In the land formerly known as Czechoslovakia, people enjoy *smažený sýr*, a thick slice of Emmental or other cheese that's breaded and fried, and often accompanied by tartar sauce. South Korea chows down on *tteokbokki* and *odeng*. *Tteokbokki* is a spicy stir-fried rice cake dish, and *odeng* is a type of fish cake. Ramen pairs well with drinking in Japan. It's not the plain bowl of dorm-room noodles but comes with all the toppings, like you see in anime. *Acarajé* is a traditional street food found in Brazil; these black-eyed pea fritters are often served with a shrimp paste center. While all these foods sound great, the award for King of Drunk Food goes to Scotland for creating the Munchy Box—a pizza box filled fried, greasy drunk foods, like fried chicken, pizza, kebab meat, onion rings, fries, garlic bread, and, if you are lucky, a deep-fried Mars bar.

The Morning After

After a night on the town, you will need something to keep body and soul together the next morning. You can load up on protein with an English breakfast, also called a fry-up or a full English. Stumble over to a huge plate of bacon, sausage, eggs, mushrooms, tomatoes, and baked beans. It may not be the healthiest meal, but it has nutrients you need, as well as the grease you crave.

The light fare of French pastries and fruit is called a Continental breakfast, because it's the opposite of the English breakfast.

If soup feels more your speed, try Korean *haejangguk*. *Haejangguk* is a catch-all term for Korean soups, or guk, eaten to cure a hangover. The most common variety is made of beef broth with pork, vegetables, and ox blood. Congealed ox blood. In little cubes. Maybe we will stick to *phở* in Vietnam, a hearty, spicy soup filled with beef, noodles, lime, basil, and bean sprouts. Phở is thought to be an effective hangover cure because the liquid broth helps to fight dehydration. Having a monosyllabic name while your brain is barely functional does not hurt, either.

A bowl of phở.

In Senegal, the traditional hangover soup is *jassa*, a citrusy chicken stew. Most recipes emphasize the importance of letting the chicken marinade in a variety of spices before cooking. The spiciness is thought to revitalize you, but it does require you begin the dish before you go out drinking. *Levanta muertos* is the pork stew Bolivians use to bounce back from a brutal hangover; its name means "raising from the dead." Made with pork, cumin, garlic, and potato, this stew follows the pattern of hearty and spicy dishes. Another well-named hangover food is tiger toast, Australian grilled cheese with stripes of Vegemite. If you are suffering in Turkey, get some *kokoreç*, grilled sheep intestines, chopped up with tomatoes and peppers. The Japanese answer to hangovers is *miso* soup with *shijimi* clams. These clams contain ornithine, an amino acid that helps the liver function to remove toxins. When Russians are faced with a hangover, they reach for *rassol*, a pungent juice that comes from pickled sauerkraut and helps to replenish electrolytes and fluids lost from over-imbibing. *Rassol* can also be made into *rassolnik* soup, with beef, barley, and herbs to downplay the pickle flavor.

Take Comfort

A number of these foods get the designation of "drunk food" or "hangover food" because they are also favorite comfort foods. Take for instance the Spanish tortilla, which is distinctly different from a Mexican tortilla. Not quite an omelet per se, *tortilla Española* consists of sautéed potato and onion baked into eggs, served warm or at room temperature. Mexican *chilaquiles* are lightly fried corn tortillas that are quartered, cooked with salsa or mole, and topped with pulled chicken, Mexican crema, queso fresco, eggs, and refried beans. Spicy, crunchy, and creamy all in one bite, it's a comforting dish that's as satisfying as it's versatile. *Oden* is a Japanese winter dish typically made of boiled eggs, radish, *konjac*, fish cakes, and broth. Different households and regions make their own variations by adding fish, beef, vegetables, or tofu to the hearty hot-pot meal. *Pão de queijo*, Brazilian cheese bread, are small rolls, served as snacks and breakfast. Starchy dough baked with milk, eggs, and cheese gives the bread its unique texture that's crispy on the outside and tender and chewy on the inside.

Pão de queijo: the tastiness cannot be overstated.

Cha siu bao, or barbecue pork buns, are a common dish served in Cantonese dim sum. The dense, yet soft dough is filled with slow-roasted marinated pork tenderloin. *Khichdi*, a risotto-like Indian dish of rice and lentils, is light, filling, and nutritious. This one-pot meal is often flavored with vegetables and spices like curry leaves, turmeric, and cumin. Poland's preference is *pierogis*, noodle dumplings stuffed with onions, mashed potatoes, sauerkraut, ground meat, cheese, or even fruit, then boiled, baked, or fried. Moussaka, often described as Greek lasagna, is prepared with layers of sautéed eggplant, topped with minced lamb, chopped tomatoes, onion, garlic, and spices.

A WORLD OF PIZZA

Pizza Starter

For someone born in the current generation, it strains the imagination to think that yogurt, bagels, and pizza were once considered "ethnic" foods. It would be hard to imagine our lives without foods like these, especially pizza. Early forms of pizza were most likely a flatbread called *focaccia*, with one or two toppings. The word "pizza" was first documented in 997 CE in Central and Southern Italy. There was no tomato sauce, since tomatoes are a New World food that did not reach Italy until the sixteenth century. The addition of mozzarella cheese did not come on the scene until the nineteenth century. Proper mozzarella cheese is made from the milk of cape buffalo, which looks like a water buffalo and nothing like a bison. According to legend, these ingredients were first combined when King Umberto I and Queen Margherita visited Naples in 1889. Chef Raffaele Esposito combined tomato sauce, mozzarella slices and basil leaves to honor the red, white, and green of the Italian flag and named it Pizza Margherita, in honor of the queen. It was lucky for him, and all of us, that the queen enjoyed his pizza most of all the ones she tried.

Italian immigrants would bring pizza to the United States, but it initially stayed in their neighborhoods in the Northeast. The first documented pizzeria in the US was G. Lombardi's on Spring Street in Manhattan, licensed to sell pizza in 1905. (Whatever you do, do not get involved in the debate of which

NYC pizzeria was the first, and the less said about New York versus Chicago style, the better.) Pizza did not gain widespread popularity until soldiers returning from tours in Italy during World War II brought back a hankering for the pizza they enjoyed in Naples. In the 1940s, sales of oregano increased by 5,200 percent due to the surge in popularity of pizza and other Italian foods. In 1957, the Celentano Brothers marketed the first frozen pizza.

Hawaiian pizza was invented in Canada by a Greek man, is based on Chinese flavors, and is the most popular pizza in Australia.

Hawaiian pizza is guaranteed to start an argument in a group of five or more people.

International Pie

Today, pizza can be found in nearly every corner of the globe, even though globes are round and utterly lacking in corners. You could tour the world eating only pizza and never eat it the same way twice. Every country and culture modified this disc of deliciousness to their own tastes. Those readers who get nauseous or angry thinking about pineapple on pizza may want to skip this section. Australians like to add shrimp to Hawaiian pizzas. Brazilians top their pies with hard boiled eggs and peas. Germany likes their pizza with eggs sunny side up. Why not? It works on burgers and hash. Costa Rica likes coconut. People in China have a penchant for thousand island dressing and eel, though not necessarily together. India tops theirs with chicken tikka, which isn't a native food but an import from the UK. Reindeer is a common meat for Finnish pies. Koreans top theirs with sweet potatoes and crab. Pizza changes the most when served in Asian countries where tomatoes are not common, and most people are lactose intolerant. Spicy sausages and cured meats are major players in Turkey. Venezuela goes *elotes*-style, by adding corn and goat cheese. Japan favors squid and Mayo Jaga, a combination of mayonnaise, potatoes, and bacon that's a street food staple. Russian like *mockba*, a blend of sardines, tuna, salmon, mackerel, and onions. There is one country whose preference I do not think I could bring myself to try. Our friends in Sweden top theirs with ham, curry powder, and bananas. Mushy, hot bananas.

> In 2009, the European Union declared Neapolitan pizza a heritage food. All pizzerias selling "Neapolitan pizza" must comply with strict rules on ingredients and preparation, including using only San Marzano tomatoes and fresh buffalo mozzarella. This protected status enables producers to boast about their exclusivity and charge a premium for the pizza.

Close Enough

The category of pizza topping preferences is extensive, even if we only confine it to things called "pizza." You would be hard-pressed to find a culture in the world without a flatbread, whether plain or topped. Georgian *khackapuri* is wrapped around cheese, then topped with an egg and a generous dollop of butter. *Manakish* in Lebanon is made with *za'atar*, a spicy mixture of thyme, sesame seeds, and sumac. *Chapati* is a whole wheat flatbread native to South Asia and parts of Africa, used to pick up bits of meat and vegetables or to sop up soups, stews, and curries. Frybread is a Native American flatbread that's fried in oil or lard. This is a relatively new tradition, having started in 1864 when the US government gave provisions to the Navajo people that included flour. Frybread is eaten as a side dish, wrapped like a taco, or smothered with honey or jam. The Czech side of my family cherishes our *pagachi*, a flatbread with mashed potatoes inside and brown butter and chives on top. (Only six of us know how to make it and only two are any good at it.) *Lavash* is a large, unleavened Armenian flatbread that's cooked against the hot walls of a clay oven, similar to the way Indian *naan* is cooked in a *tandoori*. *Lavash* is soft and flexible when fresh, but dries to a brittle state, at which point it can be stored for months. Ethiopia uses an ancient grain called teff to make *injera*, a spongy flatbread. Somalia has *sabaayad* and Morocco has *r'gafe*. Do not forget the more familiar friends, like matzoh and pita.

Crusty Cousins

We need only broaden the definition of "flatbread" a little to see that everyone is invited to the table. Russia has blintzes, China has wontons, and Mexico has tortillas. If you wrap those unleavened flatbreads around something, you get another universal food, the dumpling. Savory offerings could be *xioalongbao* in China, *gyoza* in Japan, *pierogies* in Poland, ravioli and tortellini in Italy, *kartoffelknoedel* in Germany, empanadas in Mexico, *pitepalt* from Sweden, pasties from Cornwall in the UK, *pastelles* in Trinidad and Tobago, *papas rellena* in Cuba, knish of eastern Europe's Ashkenazi Jews, *mandu* in Korea, *tiropitakia* in Greece, *balhinas de carne* in Brazil, *momo* in Nepal, samosas in India, *khinkali* in Georgia, and *pelmini, cheburek, and piroski* from Russia. That's only confining ourselves to filled dumplings. Dropped or rolled dumplings include *manti* in Khazakstan, *bryndzové halušky* in Slovakia, *spetzle* in Germany, gnocchi in Italy, and naturally the dumplings of chicken & dumplings fame. That would lead us into pasta and noodles, but you get the point.

Japanese gyoza.

THE REAL COST OF FOOD

You are being more responsible with your eating and your money, so tonight you are going to make hamburgers instead of getting drive-through. It's a good thought and a sensible practice, but there are costs to our food that reach far beyond what comes up on the cash register display: costs that no coupon can reduce.

Meat Is Murder on the Environment

Meat is responsible for 14.5 percent of greenhouse gas emissions. Rearing livestock for animal-based products requires more land, water, and energy than producing grain. Twenty-seven kilograms of CO_2 is generated per kilogram of beef, compared to 0.9 kilograms per kilogram of lentils. For comparison, the average car today emits about 0.4 kilograms of CO_2 per mile driven. In addition, poor handling of manure and fertilizers can degrade local water resources, while unsustainable farming practices can lead to the loss of ecologically important areas, such as prairies, wetlands, and forests. Let's go through the barnyard and look at the greenhouse gas emissions that result from raising terrestrial animals for food on a commercial scale.

Costly and adorable.

Mary had a little lamb, each kilogram of which resulted in thirty-nine kilograms of CO_2, equivalent to driving about ninety miles. Half of the lamb eaten in the US is imported, so some of its carbon footprint comes from shipping. Most of the CO_2 is produced by the animals' digestion (a.k.a. lamb farts), their feed, manure management, and other farm operations. Flatulence of greenhouse gases is a major issue with beef cattle, whose production creates twenty-seven kilograms of CO_2 per kilo of meat. They also require a great deal of water and land, both to live on and to grow their feed.

Half as bad, but still not good is the CO_2 of pork, at twelve kilograms per kilo of meat. More than half of the emissions from pork come from raising the animals, but a good portion comes from processing, transporting, and cooking the meat at home. The Thanksgiving holiday is many things, but environmentally conscious isn't among them. Turkeys come at a cost of eleven kilograms of CO_2, largely from feed production, especially corn, followed by processing and home cooking. Which came first, the chicken or the egg? On a descending list of carbon emission, it's the chicken. (The actual answer to that question is the egg, by the way.) Chickens produce the least greenhouse gas emissions of most popular types of meat at seven kilograms. At 4.8 kilos, eggs are probably your best choice of animal protein if you want to reduce your carbon footprint. Most of the emissions come from feed production for the laying hens, on-farm energy use, nitrous oxide gas from the poultry litter, and fuel combustion.

> Dairy isn't much better. A seven ounce glass of milk brings with it twenty-one ounces (or 0.6 kilograms) of greenhouse gases from the world's 270 million dairy cows.

Dairy-free Dread

You may have heard online, repeatedly and vehemently, that the planet could be saved if everyone went vegan. According to a 2016 Oxford study, the adoption of a vegan diet globally would cut food-related emissions by 70 percent. Of course, it's not as simple as that. While a worldwide diet of plants that might solve some animal-based problems, it would create others.

Growing more fruits, vegetables, and grains means more land must be cleared, removing the native plants that evolved to grow there. Those grasses and trees are also home to rodents, deer, birds, and other creatures that are killed to protect food crops. Some crops are especially devastating to native species, such as palm oil, the commercial cultivation of which has been responsible for the near annihilation of orangutans, pygmy elephants, Sumatran elephants, and tigers.

A popular vegan substitution for dairy is cashews. Cashews are rich in minerals like iron, zinc, magnesium, protein, fiber, and heart-healthy monounsaturated fat. Leaving aside the carbon footprint of shipping, the unexpected cost that comes with cashews is a human one. A cashew is technically not a nut at all, but closer to a seed or bean, harvested from the cashew apple. Two hard shells have to be removed to get to the cashew, which contain harmful cardol and anacardic acid. No machine has yet been devised that can do this effectively and safely, so it must be done by hand. Cashews grow in countries like Vietnam, Nigeria, and India, nations not famous for safe working conditions. Many workers in the cashew industry, who have been reported to earn as little as $2.60 per day, suffer with debilitating burns to their hands from the acids in the shells because they are not provided with gloves. As if that were not enough, according to a 2011 Human Rights Watch report, cashews are processed in forced labor camps in Vietnam, which led to the use of the term "blood cashews."

Almonds are the source of the bestselling nondairy milk, but almonds are even more thirsty than we are. It takes a gallon of water to produce a single almond. A half-gallon carton of almond milk is made from two cups of almonds. At approximately 125 almonds to the cup, that equals 250 gallons of water per half-gallon of almond milk. This water consumption is a particular problem in drought-stricken California, where more than 80 percent of the world's almonds are grown. Commercial almond production has required diverting ground and surface waters from the state's aqueduct system for irrigation. This year-round crop consumes about 8 to 10 percent of the area's agricultural water supply. So much water is being consumed that the floor of the San Joaquin Valley had sunk twenty-eight feet (or 8.5 meters) since the 1920s due to groundwater depletion.

Many almonds are being grown on land that has been converted from natural lands, including 16,000 acres of wetlands or farms growing low-water crops, to meet the rising demand. Another significant problem is pesticide use, which is contaminating limited water sources and contributing to the toxification of drinking water for people in California's farming communities. According to the Pesticide Action Network, the USDA Pesticide Data Program has found residues of nine different pesticides on almonds, five of which are toxic to honeybees, posing yet another threat to the environment.

Soy *Intranquilo*

The classic alternative to meat is soy. For soybeans to be economically viable, large swathes of land are needed to grow them. As a result, ecosystems throughout South America, especially in the Amazon rainforest of Brazil, have suffered extreme deforestation, with as much as 9.9 million acres of forests being destroyed annually. Satellite imagery showed that the expansion of cropland, mainly for soy, was the main driver of deforestation between 2001 and 2004. The biodiverse Cerrado Basin in Brazil, the world's second largest producer of soybeans, has been hit especially hard. Cerrado is home to around 5 percent of all species on Earth, including over 10,000 species of plants, almost half of which are unique to the area.

Young soybean pod.

> 70 to 75 percent of soy goes into animal feed, with the remainder split between bio-diesel production and human consumption.

Since 2006, Brazil has had a "soy moratorium," an agreement between the companies who buy nearly all the soy in Brazil not to buy any soy that had been grown on recently deforested land. The agreement also included a provision to blacklist farmers known to be using slave labor, an issue we will touch on again later. The moratorium was renewed indefinitely in 2016. However, as with most legal documents, people found a loophole. Soy fields were moved to older deforested land which was previously being used for cattle, while the cattle were moved to the newly cleared fields. Theoretically, there is also a moratorium in place against deforestation for cattle farming, but enforcement is much harder with cattle, because a herd of cows is easier to move than a field of plants. The moratorium only applies to the areas the cattle were on immediately before being sent to slaughter. This means that cattle can easily be raised on illegally cleared land and then moved to legal land at the last moment.

The demand for soybeans continues to grow, driven in part by the rising middle classes in heavily populated China and India. Meeting this demand isn't as simple as planting more soybeans. Soy is an annual crop and one that is resistant to fertilizers. To increase the yield, more plants need to be grown and that requires more space. If the global demand for direct consumption and animal feed continues to grow as expected, soy production will need to increase by nearly 80 percent. The implications of this are simply catastrophic for the environment.

While soybeans were originally imported from Asia, the dramatically popular grain quinoa comes from South American. Since making the transition from "obscure offering at the local health food store" to "grocery store regular," this low-fat, high-protein superfood, which contains all nine essential amino acids, has become a watchword for healthy living. (Bear in mind, "superfood" is not a medical or scientific term. It has no set definition and no conditions on its use. "Superfood" is pure marketing.) The United Nations declared 2013 to be the International Year of Quinoa, demonstrating how the nutritious grain became a global favorite. Healthy, yes. Guilt-free, not as much. While food bloggers in Western countries tout quinoa as a superfood because of its high nutritional values, local Andean people in Bolivia and Peru can no longer afford to eat what had been an indigenous staple food for seven thousand years.

Although it's prepared like a grain, quinoa is actually a pseudo-cereal related to spinach, chard, and beets.

Quin-what?

Bolivia and Peru produce more than 80 percent of the world's quinoa, followed by Ecuador, the USA, and China. For centuries, quinoa was cultivated for domestic consumption and was considered "peasants' food" with no commercial value. In the 1970s, quinoa's high nutritional values caught the interest of American and European consumers. Demand for it rose rapidly, as did its market price. From 2000 to 2008 alone, the price of quinoa increased by 600 percent. The ever-rising prices led to increased production, as farmers hoped to cash in on the popularity. On one hand, farmers hope to benefit from the growing quinoa trade, but it makes them vulnerable at the same time. Although the rise in global demand for quinoa has brought income to certain segments of the economy, it has negatively affected the food security of the Bolivian population. The high price of quinoa encourages farmers to sell their better-quality quinoa for export and keep the less nutritious varieties for the domestic market. Furthermore, the major foods that make up the daily calories of Bolivians has shifted from quinoa to less nutritious breads and pasta.

Since Quinoa Real is the most commonly purchased and consumed type of quinoa, many farmers have turned to mono-cropping for greater profits, which threatens the genetic diversity of quinoa. The rise in production has also led to a shift from traditional, small-scale, manual farming techniques, to large-scale, mechanized methods, which brings with it reduced biodiversity and stress on the soil. For all of that, quinoa-producing countries like Bolivia remain among the poorest and most food-insecure in South America. With 80 percent of the rural population living below the poverty line, Bolivia is considered the poorest country in the Andes.

Green Gold

Like almonds, domestic avocados are primarily grown in California and require a lot of water: seventy-two gallons per pound of avocados. California avocados are only 10 percent of those eaten in the US. The rest come from Mexico, where they have earned the nickname "green gold." The highest-producing region is Michoacan, home to rich, volcanic soil, five million people, and the Zetas, a crime syndicate made up of former army commandos, among others. Michoacan endured an average of over eight hundred murders annually from 1995 to 2015. For perspective, New York City, with nearly double the population, had 290 homicides.

Mexican avocados had been banned in the US in 1914, out of fear of insect infestations and cheap competition. Before the North American Free Trade Agreement facilitated the import of foreign avocados, beginning in 1994, Americans ate about a pound of California avocados per person per year. That amount has grown by 700 percent and continues to rise. Today, avocados dominate the Michoacan economy, with nearly 60 percent of farming revenue coming directly or indirectly from "green gold." In the tiny town of Tancítaro, avocados generate more than a million dollars every day. Such sums of money were not going to escape the notice of organized crime. As early as 2007, when Michoacan became the first state in Mexico permitted by the US Department of Agriculture to send unlimited exports of avocados over the border, mobsters recognized an emerging opportunity.

One gang, La Familia Michoacana, made its entrance by tossing five rivals' heads onto a dance floor in the town of Uruapan. Next were the Knights Templar, who boasted of a chivalric code of honor, even as it extorted and kidnapped farmers and stole their land. Another group, Los Viagras, burned dozens of vehicles on the state's main highway, shutting it down. State and local police and landowners tried to fight back, but the cartels continued to grow stronger. Farmers who refused to pay protection had their orchards burned. One farmer's son was kidnapped and held for a million-dollar ransom; the farmer was himself kidnapped twice. In 2014, it was reported that the Knights Templar gang made $152 million a year from terrified farmers. Stories began filtering into Western media of pregnant teachers being murdered, but the demand for avocados continued to rise.

What have these avocados wrought?

There is a glimmer of hope for the region. The cartels did not continue completely unchecked. In late 2013, residents of Tancítaro and other small towns decided they had had enough. They took up arms, forming self-defense groups to drive the gangs out. Their equipment and training came from the state police, and their salaries were paid in part by the avocado growers and packers. Eighty heavily armed and armored residents, many of them farmers who had been extorted, patrol the farms full-time to let the cartels know they are not welcome.

Indentured Agriculture

One thing that predictably fails to come up in assertions that eating fruits and vegetables instead of meat reduces suffering is the plight of humans, who have not yet been replaced by machines in agricultural jobs. Many are undocumented aliens without legal protections, who cannot protest their work conditions or below-minimum wages. Others are literal slaves. In Mexico, the approximately three million migrant farm workers or day laborers are the most vulnerable to being pressed into forced labor, according to local and international studies. Many are tricked by middlemen, called *enganchadores*, with promises of good wages and working conditions. Once on the farms, they often work twelve or more hours per day, under the threat of physical violence. Adolescents and children work alongside the adults in the same conditions. If they are paid at all, their meager wages disappear when they are forced to buy basic necessities from the *tiendas de raya*, or company stores, like the ones that kept the people of Appalachian mining communities impoverished. If the workers cannot afford what they need, they find themselves in continuous, growing debt to the people who forbid them to leave.

There are 1.95 million victims of slave labor in the Americas, 5 percent of the world total, according to the 2018 Global Slavery Index. In the United States, 12 of every 10,000 people are forced laborers, unwilling child brides, or other people who have been stripped of their liberties. The number of forced laborers per 10,000 people rises in Latin America: 17 in Brazil, 27 in Mexico and Columbia, 37 in Cuba, and 56 in Venezuela. The situation is more dire in sub-Saharan Africa, the Middle East, and Asia, and modern slavery isn't confined to agriculture. Textiles, mining, and even electronics manufacturing benefit from the labor of people treated like property.

We did not even get into the health care costs associated with modern Western diets (86 percent of all health care spending), financial assistance for underpaid fast food workers (seven billion dollars), or the environment impact of ordering groceries online versus driving to the store yourself. So what is a person to do? Illustrious British actor and writer Stephen Fry may have summed it up best, "Everything casts a shadow in this world." All we can do is try to learn where our food and goods come from, purchase wisely, and, most importantly, make the best use of what we already have.

CHAPTER 7

People

CONCAVE EARTHERS

From Greek *Tartarus* to Hindu *Patala*, from Aztec *Mictlan* to Christian Hell, ancient or extant, myth or metaphor, almost every civilization that has even stood on Earth has had some version of an underworld. The living stay on top of the Earth, and the dead go beneath, be it a few years or eternity. Our "blue marble" is made up of layers familiar to anyone who took Earth Science in school: crust, mantle, outer core, and inner core. Beneath the soil we walk on and the rock below that, liquid magma surrounds a dense, hot core made primarily of iron and nickel. But what if the Earth did not contain those layers? What if there was nothing inside the planet at all? That was the theory some of the world's leading scientists espoused in the seventeenth century, that the Earth is hollow.

Halley's Comment

The first person to broadly propagate the idea of a hollow Earth was someone whose name is inexorably tied to astronomy, the man who realized three reported comets were really only one comet and became that comet's namesake, Edmund Halley. In 1692, frustrated by anomalous compass readings he could not explain, Halley proposed that the planet was a series of three shells, one inside the other, which spin in different directions and at different speeds around a central core. According to his calculations of the Earth's magnetic field and the gravitational pull of the sun and the moon, this model would explain away the inaccuracies of his compass readings. While he was on the topic, he posited that the spaces between the shells could have atmospheres capable of supporting life and that gases escaping through the outermost shell were the source of the aurora borealis. Halley's essays were popular, and while fellow scientists were intrigued by his geomagnetic data, few were keen on his hollow Earth theory.

As Bad as It Symmes

For the next few hundred years, the hollow Earth idea floated around, changing slightly with each adherent, like a geological game of telephone. Over time, the concentric shells gave way to an entirely hollow globe, with the core being a small sun that created an ideal living environment inside. The idea had staying power, if only on the fringes of science. In 1818, John Cleves Symmes, Jr., a veteran of the War of 1812 and failed frontier trader with no apparent scientific education, published his *Circular No. 1*, pronouncing the Earth to be hollow and "stocked with thrifty vegetables and animals, if not men." Symmes wrote: "I declare the Earth is hollow, and habitable within; containing a number of solid concentrick [sic] spheres, one within the other, and that it is open at the poles twelve or sixteen degrees; I pledge my life in support of this truth, and am ready to explore the hollow, if the world will support and aid me in the undertaking."

Spoiler alert, the earth doesn't look like this.

Symmes' version of the hollow Earth theory included the unique addition of huge holes at the North and South Poles, which would come to be known as "Symmes holes," that would allow sunlight to reach the world inside.

Bonus fact: It's important not to confuse Junior with his uncle John Cleves Symmes, a delegate to the Continental Congress, father-in-law of President William Henry Harrison, and great-grandfather of President Benjamin Harrison.

Not content to theorize, Symmes went on the lecture circuit to propose an expedition to the North Pole to locate and infiltrate the Symmes hole there to prove "the existence of an inhabited concave to this globe." To hear him pitch the idea, the trek would be an easy one. Symmes claimed that navigable rivers flowed into the access portals at the poles. Sailors at the edge of one of the portals would not even feel their ship descending into the interior of the planet as undiscovered animals, and even people, were revealed. Enough people took notice, and a presumably emboldened Symmes petitioned the US Congress for "two vessels of 250 or 300 tons." He had help from a wealthy Ohio man, James McBride, and senator Richard Johnson, who would become vice president under Martin Van Buren. The trio petitioned Congress for funding for years to no avail, but President John Adams said he would approve funding in 1828. Unfortunately for the Symmes camp, Adams was succeeded by Andrew Jackson before the funding could be made official, and Jackson was, to understate it, not a fan of the idea. Symmes died that same year.

One person in whom Symmes' ideas resonated was a young newspaper editor named Jeremiah Reynolds. While Reynolds believed the Earth was hollow and accessible at the poles, the two men diverged over a stubborn disagreement over which pole would make for the best expedition. Symmes favored the North Pole, but Reynolds only wanted to mount an expedition to the South Pole. Reynolds was a more convincing public speaker than Symmes and had friendships he could leverage to get scientific groups to bombard Congress with letters of support for a government-sponsored South Pole exploration. Also striking out with the government, Reynolds joined forces with a wealthy patron to equip, provision, and man a ship for a year-long voyage. In 1929, eight years after the first man set foot on Antarctica, Reynolds and his captain, N. B. Palmer, found themselves on a land mass that was much larger than they had anticipated, certainly too large to search with no opportunity to reprovision themselves, outside of a sea lion the crew killed. Reynolds decided the opening to the Earth must be completely blocked by impassible ice, and they headed back, stopping in Chile when the crew mutinied and put Reynolds and Captain Palmer ashore. After that, Reynolds abandoned the quest to prove the hollow Earth.

Under Pressure

In his *Elements of Natural History* in 1829, physicist Sir John Leslie included an endnote describing his hollow Earth theory, based on his "theory of the compression of bodies." This theory was based on an experiment that Leslie believed established the compressibility of water. Even then, most scientists accepted what we now know, that water can't be compressed. The theory of the compression of bodies states that the density of any substance is a function of its elastic properties and its distance from Earth's center. Leslie calculated that Earth's core must be inconceivably dense, meaning Earth must be thousands of times more massive than Newtonian physics showed it to be. Accepting previous measurements of Earth's circumference, but holding fast to his density estimates, Leslie wrote, "Our planet, must have a very widely cavernous structure and we tread on a crust or shell whose thickness bears but a very small proportion to the diameter of its sphere." The concept of an absolute vacuum had yet to enter the collective mind of science, so Leslie assumed something must fill the interplanetary void. Solids, liquids, and gases would all be subject to the intense compression he believed was in play, but light would not be. "The great central concavity is not that dark and dreary abyss which the fancy of Poets had pictured. On the contrary, this spacious internal vault must contain the purest ethereal essence, Light in its most concentrated state, shining with intense refulgence and overpowering splendour." The scientific community of the day rejected Leslie's theories about hollow Earth and compression. He might have been forgotten entirely if not for Jules Verne, who credits Leslie as inspiration for *Journey to the Center of the Earth* in 1864.

We Live Inside

Cyrus Teed was an alchemist and "eclectic physician" (practitioner of botanical cures) in Utica, NY. During an 1869 experiment in "electro-alchemic research," Teed was knocked unconscious, whereupon he received a vision from "The Divine Motherhood." She told him that he was the Messiah who must redeem the human race and explained the truth of the universe, which included the Earth being hollow and mankind living inside it. When Teed came to, he adopted the name "Koresh," the Hebrew form of Cyrus, and split his energy between the hollow Earth and building a utopian community. His new motto: "We live inside."

Teed's inside-out universe was referred to as "cellular cosmogony." In his 1898 book of the same name, he explained, "The entire universe that we see in the sky lies within this cell, cradled in the hands of God." At the center of Teed's hollow, multi-layered Earth is the sun, rotating on a twenty-four-hour cycle, creating the illusion of dawn and dusk. The sun is bright on one half and dark on the other; the dark side emits light from many tiny openings, which we interpret as stars. The Earth's crust is a hundred miles thick and made up of seventeen layers. The outermost seven layers are metallic, five are minerals, and the innermost five are made of rock. The other planets in our solar system are flat discs floating between the metallic layers, while the moon is a reflection of the Earth's crust. We cannot see across to the other side of the hollow Earth, because our atmosphere is too thick. We are held to the ground by centrifugal force, not gravity. Outside our planetary cell is only the void.

For the record, this is our basic situation.

In addition to cellular cosmogony, Teed believed in reincarnation, celibacy, immortality, and collectivism, as did the people who joined him in his utopian communities. The Koreshan Unity community started in the 1870s in New York, before moving to Chicago, where their commune was called Beth-Ophra, then to San Francisco, before finally settling in Estero, Florida. Moving the community around initially did help to spread Teed's message to small pockets of a few thousand people total, somewhat less than Teed's vision of a utopian city of ten million citizens, with streets up to four hundred feet wide. "New Jerusalem" reached its peak when it had over 250 residents around 1905. The Koreshans built extensively, establishing stores, a bakery, a print shop for their writings (like the *Flaming Sword* newsletter), a power plant that supplied power to the region, and the community was extensively landscaped. They sought power in local politics with their Progressive Liberal party, but never got very far. Residents of New Jerusalem were divided into castes: nonbelievers working with the community, who are free to marry and mate; the Department of Equitable Administration, who are allowed to marry, but are only to have sex for procreation; and the celibate, communal Pre-Eminent Unity. Within each of these were secular, commercial, and educational branches. Day-to-day administration was the province of a council of women, "The Seven Sisters," who lived in a house called the Planetary Court.

Teed and some followers formed the Koreshan Geodetic Survey in 1897 to scientifically prove Earth's concavity. Phase one involved the help of an inventor named Ulysses Grant Morrow to project a horizontal line long enough to, they claimed, show the concave ground rising to meet it. Phase two required a specially constructed apparatus called a "rectilineator," that vaguely resembled a suspension bridge made of lumber and wire and functioned like a giant spirit level. If it worked, it would prove Teed's calculations that the Earth's surface curves upward at eight inches per mile was correct, and their reference line would meet the water about four miles offshore. It took a month just to construct and calibrate the rectilineator on a Naples, Florida beach. The rectilineator was only twelve feet long; the distance they were testing was over four miles long. The Geodetic Survey spent five months patiently moving and recalibrating the rectilineator along the beach. Their results proved mathematically that the Earth was concave, and Teed offered a $100,000 prize (almost three million dollars today) to anyone who could prove he was wrong. We will never know if Teed realized that the math that "proved" the Earth's surface was concave was the exact same math that proved it was convex. He maintained his theory until his death on December 22, 1908. The Koreshans, believing in reincarnation, kept his body above ground, expecting him to come back to life on Christmas day. When there was no "second coming," local authorities insisted the corpse be buried. The Koreshan Unity began to splinter and fade almost immediately, though the colony still had members as recently as 1961.

> Both Teed and Symmes have monuments in their honor—the Koreshan State Historic Site and Ohio's Hollow Earth Monument.

Third Reich from the Sun

A decade or so after Teed's death, copies of the Koreshans' *Flaming Sword* found their way into a WWI French prisoner-of-war camp and the hands of a German pilot, Peter Bender. Bender was taken with the idea of cellular cosmogony. Returning to Germany after the war, Bender developed and promoted the idea of *hohlweltlehre*, or "hollow Earth doctrine," a simplified version of Teed's theory, conspicuously devoid of religious references. *Hohlweltlehre* drew some supporters, and while mainstream scientists were not among them, Bender was able to curry enough political favor to test his theory. The first test, in 1933, was to launch a rocket straight up into the sky, to see if it hit the opposite side of the planet. The rocket failed to launch properly and crashed a short distance away. Hermann Goering, with whom Bender had some connection from his pilot days, was instrumental in getting the second test approved. German Naval Research Institute officers thought hohlweltlehre might be used to their advantage in locating enemy ships. An expedition was launched to Rugen Island in the Baltic Sea to try to use telescopic cameras pointed upwards at the supposed concavity to detect British ships. Bender claimed that the Earth's surface seems convex because of the refraction of visible light passing through the atmosphere, so the cameras were fitted with infrared filters, as infrared radiation isn't refracted in the atmosphere. If Earth's surface were concave, the infrared photographs should show the positions of British ships in the Baltic and North seas. They did not. Nazi High Command was embarrassed by the failure, and Bender, his wife, and some of his followers were sent to death camps. It bears noting that the depth to which the Nazis were truly invested in hollow Earth doctrine and the fate of Bender, et al, are contested, with some sources claiming it's "weird Nazi" apocrypha while others are steadfast on its veracity.

Does the Hollow Earth Have Wi-Fi?

It would be nice to think that belief in a hollow Earth went out with big band music, but it has persisted even into the era where 3.2 billion people have near-instant access to the collective sum of mankind's knowledge and wisdom. Beyond Halley, Symmes, and Reynolds, modern hollow Earth theory was also influenced by the 1892 novel, *The Goddess of Atvatabar, or The History of the Discovery of the Interior World*. In the plot full of what would become science fiction and fantasy tropes, the protagonist enters the interior of the globe through a Symmes hole and finds an advanced civilization whose spiritual powers are capable of everything from maintaining youth to bringing the dead back to life. The eponymous goddess falls in love with the man, a civil war breaks out over their forbidden romance, and the man becomes their new king, who then opens trade relations with the surface world.

"My conception of the Hollow Earth, based on my research is that the shell of the Earth is about eight hundred miles thick, from the outside to the inner surface," claims Rodney Cluff, author of *World Top Secret: Our Earth IS Hollow*. Like Teed, Cluff believes the hollow Earth contains a small sun with a daytime side and a nighttime side, and, like Symmes, he believes that there are large openings at the poles. While there is variation of belief across modern hollow Earth "truthers," some common themes emerge. The inside of the Earth is a tropical paradise that is home to an advanced race of beings that could be humans, aliens, giants, or some combination thereof. These people are the descendants of ancient races, the Lost Ten Tribes of Israel, or the people of Lemuria, a mythical Atlantis-like land. They are peaceful and scientifically advanced, to the point of having space travel technology. The inner-Earth climate is so perfect as to grow giant plants and animals, like trees a thousand feet tall. This inner world is sometimes called Agartha, after a legendary Earth-core city from Eastern mysticism.

If the inside of our planet is replete with giant animals and a race of large people with advanced technology, why have they never made themselves known? According to Cluff, they have, but an international banking conspiracy (a.k.a. "the Jews") has systematically suppressed the existence of Symmes holes and the hollow Earth they lead into. That's the answer to the question of any and all missing evidence for the more conspiracy minded Hollow Earther. A favorite piece of "suppressed evidence" is a supposed secret diary, belonging to Admiral Richard Byrd,[3] the first person to fly over the North and South Poles. According to this diary, Byrd's plane was intercepted by a flying saucer, which landed it remotely. On the ground, he was met by emissaries, who expressed their concern about the atomic bomb, and appointed him their ambassador to the surface world and the US government. (We will leave aside the fact that Byrd flew to the North Pole twenty-one years before the first atom bomb was dropped in WWII.)

If no other expedition had produced irrefutable proof of a hollow Earth, Cluff would have to launch an expedition himself. Voyage to the hollow Earth was set to leave from Murmansk, Moscow, in a Russian icebreaker ship in June 2007. Interested parties could buy their way in for $20,000. After a projected nine days on foot, the expedition would "travel up Hiddekel River to City of Jehu," before taking "a monorail trip to City of Eden to visit the Palace of the King of the Inner World." The itinerary contained a back-up plan in the event that they could not locate the Symmes hole: "Please note that if we are unable to find the opening, we will be returning via the New Siberian Islands to visit skeleton remains of exotic animals thought to originate from Inner Earth." For better or worse, "Voyage to the Hollow Earth" never got past the planning stages. One of the organizers died of cancer, another was killed in a plane crash, and a third was forced to withdraw after the largest investor in his company threatened to pull their financial support if he publicly persisted with his hollow Earth beliefs. These setbacks were also blamed on the international banking conspiracy. Subsequent attempts met with the

---

3   There is some fairly hot contention that Byrd was not only not the first person to fly over the North Pole, he did not fly over it at all, but that's a topic for another section.

same results. Still, Cluff wasn't deterred. "There are tons of people who have expressed interest in this expedition if we can get it off the ground. I don't think there is a lot of people out there, certainly not in the millions but maybe in the thousands."

AND THE LITTLE CHILD SHALL LEAD THEM

Emma Gonzalez and David Hogg are strident gun control advocates and the activists behind the March for Our Lives, despite being in their teens. Gun control might not have been the passion project they would have chosen. That was until a gunman murdered seventeen people at Marjory Stoneman Douglas High School in Parkland, Florida on February 14, 2018. Rather than shrink away and worry about themselves, the survivors of Parkland were driven to action. Even in the face of a government reluctant to change, vapid "thoughts and prayers," and ridiculous conspiracy theories that they are paid actors, Gonzalez, Hogg, and many others have fought to make sure no one else has to experience what they did. And they are not the only ones.

Iqbal Masih

Born into a poor Christian family in Punjab, Pakistan, in 1983, Iqbal Masih was sent to work for a carpet weaving business from whose owner his father had borrowed six hundred rupees (about $8.60). The terms of the agreement placed him in servitude until the debt was paid. This system of bonded slavery was called *peshgi*. He and the other children working there were chained to the looms to stop them from escaping. The factory was cramped and hot; injuries and beating were commonplace. Masih worked sixteen hours a day, with one half hour break, six days a week, for sixty rupees a day. He was fined for mistakes and use of the tools he was working with, while the loan accrued interest and his family continued to borrow. Six years later, the loan was 30,000 rupees.

At age ten, Masih learned that the bonded labor he was subjected to had been outlawed, even though it was commonly done. There may be as many as twenty million bonded laborers and child laborers; half a million children are employed in the carpet trade alone. Masih and some other children escaped and went to the police. The police, however, returned them to the factory to collect a "finder's fee" from the owner. At twelve, Masih escaped again and found a rally held by Bonded Labour Liberation Front, whose posters he has seen during his first escape. There, he learned about the rights he was supposed to have as a laborer, and that the government had canceled all debts incurred by businesses, so that the businesses must free anyone indebted to them. Precious few businesses had actually released their slaves, though. When organizers asked if anyone else wanted to speak, Masih got up and told his story. BLLF immediately mobilized to free Masih and the other slaves of the carpet factory.

Masih was able to attend a school run by BLLF for former child slaves and completed his coursework in half the time. He hoped to be a lawyer when he grew up, to use the law to protect children from forced labor. In the meantime, Masih helped to free over three thousand Pakistani children from bonded slavery and made speeches about child labor around the world. Even though he was tiny, and often sick from his life of malnutrition, Masih was a natural leader. He became involved in demonstrations and snuck into factories, pretending to work there, so he could question the children about their working conditions. This was a dangerous undertaking, but the information he gathered would help the BLLF shut the factory down, freeing the children.

In 1994, Masih flew to America to accept the Reebok Human Rights Award in Boston. "I am one of those millions of children who are suffering in Pakistan through bonded labor and child labor," he said in his acceptance speech, "but I am lucky that due to the efforts of Bonded Labour Liberation Front, I go out in freedom and I am standing in front of you here today.... BLLF have done the same work that Abraham Lincoln did for the slaves of America. Today, you are free, and I am free too." Brandeis University offered Masih a full scholarship when he was ready for college.

Back in Pakistan, while riding bikes with two cousins he was visiting on Easter Sunday, twelve-year-old Iqbal Masih was murdered by a man with a shotgun. The killer was quickly identified, but his motive remained a contentious mystery. Masih had received death threats from people in the Pakistani carpet industry, and BLLF believed one of them had hired the murder to protect their financial interests. Other people claimed that the boys had caught two men in amorous congress with a donkey, some say the motive was religious, and still others said the shooting was an accident.

Masih's short, hard life and his death were not in vain. His indomitable spirit has inspired others to fight child labor. More than twenty schools in Pakistan have been opened in his honor, one of which was funded by seventh graders in Massachusetts that Masih had spoken to about his life. The US Department of Labor created the Iqbal Masih Award for the Elimination of Child Labor, and the University of Salamanca in Spain declared April 16 to be Day Against Child Slavery in his name, among many other overtures in other countries.

Autumn Peltier

In March 2018, a thirteen-year-old girl stepped onto a stool so she could be seen over the podium at the UN General Assembly during the launch of its International Decade for Action on Water for Sustainable Development. "No one should have to worry if the water is clean or if they will run out of water," Autumn Peltier of the Anishinaabe First Nation tribe said. "No child should grow up not knowing what clean water is or never know what running water is. We all have a right to this water as we need it—not just rich people, all people." The UN estimated that more than two billion people live without safe drinking water in their homes. Peltier was invited to speak as the "representative of civil society," alongside the UN Secretary General and other dignitaries.

"Many people don't think water is alive or has a spirit. My people believe this to be true. Our water deserves to be treated as human, with human rights. We need to acknowledge our waters with personhood, so we can protect our waters."

Peltier's speech, which she spent three days writing, almost did not happen. Autumn's mother thought the email from the UN was a scam and nearly deleted it. Their flight from Toronto to New York was canceled not once, not twice, but three times, so they drove the fifteen hours from their home in the Wikwemikong Unceded Territory in Ontario to New York City.

Peltier said she was not nervous before her address, "I felt like they all wanted to hear what I had to say, and I felt heard." This was not her first experience speaking to high-ranking people. A year earlier, she was chosen to speak to Prime Minister Justin Trudeau at the Assembly of First Nations' annual winter meeting. She presented Trudeau with a ceremonial copper bowl to symbolize his responsibility to protect the country's water. Not one to get stage fright, Peltier told him firmly, "I am very unhappy with the choices you've made," referring to various pipeline projects he had supported, despite protests from environmentalists and indigenous communities, who had been under a water advisory for more than a year at that point.

Peltier had already established herself as an advocate for clean water, attending 2015 Children's Climate Conference in Sweden, and was nominated for the Children's International Peace Prize in 2017. She draws inspiration from her strong sense of cultural identity and family, like her great-aunt, Josephine Mandamin, who walked over 15,000 miles (or 25,000 kilometers) along the shorelines of the Great Lakes, Canada's largest natural resource, to bring attention to the need to protect them.

"What I've been told through ceremonies is Mother Earth has been surviving for millions of years without us. And it's taken us less than a century to destroy her—and Mother Earth doesn't need us, but we need her. One day I will be an ancestor, and I want my great-grandchildren to know I tried hard to fight, so they can have clean drinking water."

The youngest person to address the UN was ten-year-old Talya Özdemir of Turkey, who spoke on the importance of encouraging girls to pursue STEM careers in 2017.

Nkosi Johnson

Nkosi Xolani was born in an area of South Africa hit particularly hard by HIV/AIDS in 1989. His mother Daphne had passed HIV to him, and his life expectancy was short, like that of 70,000 other South African children. When Nkosi was two, already unusually old for an HIV-infected baby, Daphne could no longer care for herself and her child, and the pair was admitted to a care center in Johannesburg. That was where they met volunteer Gail Johnson. Knowing that her condition was grave, Daphne agreed that Gail would be Nkosi's foster mother.

The newly formed Johnson family had as normal a life as possible, until it was time to put Nkosi in school when he was eight, the same year his mother died. Gail had been honest about Nkosi's status when filling out the enrollment forms; they never hid his HIV status or accepted shame for it. The school stalled on admitting Nkosi and held a meeting of faculty and parents, who were evenly divided in a vote on whether to allow him to attend. The school refused to admit Nkosi. The South African constitution forbids discrimination on the grounds of medical status, so Gail took their situation public. Enough outcry was raised that the school was forced to reverse its decision, allowing Nkosi and other HIV/AIDS-afflicted children to attend.

In 1999, Gail and Nkosi founded Nkosi's Haven, a residential community offering care and support for low-income HIV/AIDS infected mothers and children, and children orphaned by AIDS, regardless of their own status. Children have access to education and therapy programs, and mothers who are able can become employees.

At eleven years old, "half the size of nothing" as Gail described him, Nkosi was the keynote speaker before 10,000 attendees of the International AIDS Conference in 2000.

"When I grow up, I want to lecture to more and more people about AIDS, and, if mommy Gail will let me, around the whole country.... You can't get AIDS if you touch, hug, kiss, hold hands with someone who is infected. Care for us and accept us. We are all human beings. We are normal. We have hands. We have feet. We can walk, we can talk, we have needs just like everyone else. Don't be afraid of us."

Nkosi did not fear death, but he felt guilty about leaving Gail. He was able to fight back against AIDS-related infections before finally succumbing at age twelve. At the time of his death, he was the longest-surviving HIV-positive-born child. Nkosi posthumously received the International Children's Peace Prize in 2005, which came with a monetary award of $100,000 for Nkosi's Haven. Nelson Mandela referred to Nkosi as an "icon of the struggle for life."

> A fourteen-year-old girl from Hong Kong, Emma Yang, developed a face-recognition app to help her grandmother and other Alzheimer's sufferers to identify people in photos and remember who they are.

Kesz Valdez

21 percent of the population of the Philippines lives below the national poverty line, with 7 percent unable to meet their basic food needs. This was life for Kesz Valdez and his family in the capital city of Manila. At age two, his abusive father forced him to collect garbage to earn money. His family tried unsuccessfully to sell him. At age four, he ran away from home, lived in a dumpsite, and slept in a graveyard. When he was five, another child pushed Valdez into a tire fire, giving him third degree burns on his back. His father refused to help him in any way, believing the boy was a jinx to the family, but Valdez's mother took him to the home of Harnin Manalaysay, who ran a mobile school for street children. Manalaysay tended Valdez's wounds, provided him with clothes, food, and an education, and became his legal guardian after Valdez's family refused to accept him back.

Valdez was thrived. "Falling into the fire left me seriously injured...but it has also been my salvation. I used to know nothing; I thought it was perfectly normal to have festering wounds on your feet. I've learned a lot since moving here." For his seventh birthday (it took some research to figure out his birthdate), Valdez asked to give presents to other children on the street, instead of having presents for himself. He and Manalaysay spent the day giving toys, candy, and slippers to other street children, many of whom had no shoes. This became an annual tradition that led to the creation of the Championing Community Children charity and the Gift of Hope program. Valdez was an inspiration to others, and a gesture that began with seven boxes of gifts ballooned into thousands of boxes.

Having been on the street, Valdez knew what street children would need to survive. Living in dumps and near open sewers, without access to health care or even hygiene, they were vulnerable to disease. Valdez made it a priority to teach them how to stay clean, brush their teeth, and care for their wounds as best they can. The children are also trained to teach these skills to other children—"Our health is our wealth! Being healthy will enable you to play, to think clearly, to get up and go to school, and love the people around you in so many ways." In 2012, at age thirteen, Valdez was awarded the International Children's Peace Prize, along with $130,000 for Championing Community Children.

SWISS ARMY WIFE

Take a Seat

It's not uncommon, across the world and throughout history, for a woman who has been widowed to take over her husband's business. That's easily done with a store or a farm, but what if your late husband earned his bread in the US Congress? Surprisingly, there is a protocol known as "widow's succession" or "widow's mandate." "Widow's succession used to be *the* way that women got into Congress, with very few exceptions," explains Debbie Walsh of the Center for American Women and Politics at Rutgers University. Not dissimilar from a queen regent ruling until the heir came of age, the idea behind the practice was continuity, the notion that the women would complete the work their husbands started. It was not a blue-moon occurrence, either. Forty-seven women have taken over their husband's seat, eight in the Senate and thirty-nine in the House. Neither was it an old-timey system that has been long forgotten. The practice actually peaked in the mid-twentieth century, and, at the time of this writing, two widows are still serving. "There was a period when you could look at all the women serving in Congress, and a majority had initially gotten in that way," says Walsh. In most cases, wives govern similarly to their husbands, though there have been notable exceptions, like California's Mary Bono, who was significantly more conservative than her late husband, Sonny. The greatest ideological differences occurred in the 1920s and 1930s, when the widows tended to govern more moderately than their husbands had.

First Lady Regent

Let's say, hypothetically, your husband had not died, but had instead been incapacitated by a stroke. And, for the sake of argument, he was not a Congressman, but the president of the United States. In October 1919, First Lady Edith Wilson unofficially ran the US government in lieu of the twenty-eighth president. In the aftermath of World War I, President Woodrow Wilson suffered a series of medical crises, culminating in a stroke that permanently paralyzed the left side of his body, blinding his left eye. While he was bedridden for the next two months, only his wife, his physicians, and a few close associates were allowed to see him.

The First Lady (and unofficial leader of the United States).

The First Lady effectively took over many of the presidential duties, including reviewing various important matters of state. She would not even consider having her husband resign and forsake his dedication to his office. The first move in establishing what she called her "stewardship" was to mislead the entire nation, from the Cabinet to the press, by only permitting an acknowledgment that Woodrow badly needed rest. When Cabinet members came to confer the president, they could go no further than the First Lady. If they had policy papers or pending decisions for him to review, edit, or approve, she would first look over the material. If she deemed the matter pressing enough, she took the paperwork into her husband's room and closed the door. As bizarre as the scenario seems, officials waited in the hallway. When she came back to them, after conferring with the president, Mrs. Wilson turned over their paperwork, now riddled with indecipherable margin notes that she said were the president's transcribed verbatim responses.

This is how she described the process, "I, myself, never made a single decision regarding the disposition of public affairs. The only decision that was mine was what was important, and what was not, and the very important decision of when to present matters to my husband." Luckily, the nation faced no great crisis for the year and five months of her stewardship. Those seventeen months did not go totally smoothly. When she heard that the Secretary of State had convened a Cabinet meeting without Wilson's permission, she considered it an act of insubordination and he was fired.

Conquering Conquistadors

Half a world away and four centuries earlier, a Mapuche woman named Janequeo led her fallen husband's troops into battle. The Mapuche are a tribe native to Chile, who, like the other tribes of the New World, found themselves besieged by Spanish conquistadors. The Mapuche had held the Spanish off for decades, thanks to their strong forts, one of which was captained by Janequeo's husband, Huepotean. Like many of their people, Huepotean was captured by the Spanish, tortured, and killed. The news of his death filled Janequeo with rage, which she focused to lead her people in retaking the fort from the Spanish and gathering an army of thousands. Not merely a tactician or figurehead, Janequeo was a fierce and skilled warrior, personally defeating a Spanish commander, whose head she mounted on her spear. The Spanish doubled and redoubled their efforts, bringing all available military might to bear on the Mapuche. Eventually, Janequeo and her army were forced to abandon their mountain fort and flee into the jungle. That is where Janequeo passes out of history and into legend, but the Mapuche continued their fight. They were able to resist conquest until the 1880s.

Mistress and Commander

We do not know how old Janequeo was when she took command of her army, but we do know the age of one Mary Patten when she took control of her ailing husband's clipper ship in 1856. She was nineteen years old. And pregnant. Though it was rarely done and often thought to be bad luck for a woman to be aboard, Patten was allowed to accompany her husband Joshua on his voyages as captain of the merchant clipper *Neptune's Car*. She used the long days at sea wisely, studying medicine and navigation. Joshua was already unwell when he was forced to order the first mate placed under arrest for dereliction of duty, which left him to do the work of two people. When he could no longer captain the ship, Patten took over for him. She set the course and navigated the vessel. She also nursed Joshua, at one point shaving his head to reduce his fever. During rough seas, she had to tie him into his bunk while she carried out the navigator's duties.

The first mate tried to persuade Patten to release him from the brig. When that failed, he tried to persuade the crew to mutiny against her and Joshua. Patten was able to convince them to remain loyal to their captain. The journey from New York to San Francisco took the *Neptune's Car* 130 days, during which Patten nursed Joshua through a second illness. Once they reach the port, Patten became an instant celebrity, and received a $1,000 bonus (at least $25,000 now) from the shipping line for her heroics. Patten said she had performed "only the plain duty of a wife towards a good husband."

The Lioness of Brittany

Where one ship helped Mary Patten care for her husband, it took many ships to help Jeanne de Clisson avenge hers. Born in 1300 to a wealthy and influential noble family in Bretton, France, Jeanne was married at age twelve to a man with whom she had two children. After her first husband's death, she married Olivier III de Clisson, and they had five children together.

Since their wealth was substantial, Olivier was enlisted by a friend to help defend Bretton against the forces of English sympathizer John de Montfort. During the Breton War of Succession, Olivier came under suspicion of treason. In 1343, the French arrested, tried, and sentenced Olivier to death by beheading. News of her husband's death ignited a great rage in Jeanne de Clisson. Her revenge against French nobility, military, and King Philip VI began with a visit to a fort her husband had once commanded. The new captain recognized her and opened the gate, but de Clisson was not alone. Her troops stormed the fort. By the time the crown sent reinforcements, the fort was burning. de Clisson sold all their lands and holdings, raising enough funds to create her soon-to-be-infamous "Black Fleet." With these ships, she attacked French ships under the cover of fog in the English Channel. News of the arrival of "Lioness of Brittany" quickly spread across the Europe.

The Black Fleet was eventually overtaken. De Clisson escaped in a rowboat with her children. Did I forget to mention she had her children with her? She rowed the boat for five days and nights until they reached England. Impressed with her power and having no love for France, King Edward III gave her more ships, and Jeanne set out again. Her quest for revenge continued with the same intensity, even after King Philip VI died in 1350. In 1356, after thirteen years of piracy and for reasons not in evidence, Jeanne de Clisson retired from her career in vengeance and lived the rest of her days in England, getting married for a third time.

Alma Reville Presents

A husband need not die for his wife to help him do his job. Some of cinema's most iconic movies would not be what they are if not for a spouse in the editing room. Take the work of Alfred Hitchcock. Alma Reville was arguably the only person to whom Hitchcock would defer to in the film-making process and usually not easily. Having begun her career at age sixteen, Reville was already an experienced editor and continuity girl (a real job title back then) when she met Hitchcock. Their working relationship began when he was made assistant director of the movie *Woman to Woman* and wanted her as editor. The salary they offered Reville was so low that she literally walked away from the project, only to have Hitchcock race down the corridor after her to make her a better offer. They would marry three years later.

For the ground-breaking movie *Psycho*, Hitchcock wanted no music in the famous shower scene, only the sounds of running water and actress Janet Leigh's screams. It was Reville who convinced him that the staccato strings of composer Bernard Herrmann were the right choice. Reville also caught a few frames that had gotten past everyone else and may have undermined the impact of the whole scene—when Leigh was laying supposedly dead in the tub, you could clearly see her swallow.

> The *Psycho* shower scene was fairly tame to shoot. It was Reville's editing that made it so intense. Leigh was so alarmed when she saw the first screening that she never took a shower again if she could avoid it.

Unbelievably, Hitchcock never won an Oscar for directing, but he did receive the American Film Institute's Lifetime Achievement Award at age seventy-nine. In his acceptance speech, he said, "I beg to mention by name only four people who have given me the most affection, appreciation, encouragement, and constant collaboration. The first of the four is a film editor, the second is a scriptwriter, the third is the mother of my daughter, Pat, and the fourth is as fine a cook as ever performed miracles in a domestic kitchen. And their names are Alma Reville."

The Cutting Room Floor

The personal relationship of working duo Marcia Lucas and her husband George was not so rosy, even though her work editing *Star Wars* made it the film that launched a media empire. Marcia was the only Lucas to bring home an Oscar, along with fellow editors Paul Hirsch and Richard Chew. Like Alma Reville, Marcia was an accomplished film editor in her own right, working under the likes of Martin Scorsese. George Lucas' original cut of the film was not the space opera fairy tale we know and love today. The opening text crawl was painfully long, the pacing was slogging, the plot was unclear, it was bloated with unnecessary backstory, there were jokes where jokes did not fit, and the focus shifted in ways that made no sense. Marcia and company rearranged the scenes to create tension where it was needed, trimmed redundant exposition, improved the pace, and gave the audience the right amount of information. It was even Marcia's idea for Obi Wan Kenobi to die. George Lucas did not win any of the Oscars he was nominated for, but Marcia Lucas, Hirsch, and Chew won for Best Editing. George and Marcia Lucas divorced in 1983, and Marcia became a minor footnote in the history of the franchise, rarely mentioned and never quoted. There is conjecture that George worked to repress her contributions. For example, he put scenes back in that she had taken out, like the scene with Han Solo and Jabba the Hutt at Mos Isley, which is one more reason to hate that scene.

Get Out of Her Heming-Way

Not every creative husband appreciates their equally creative wife, and not everyone appreciates the amazing person their partner is. Martha Gellhorn was a war correspondent reporting on the Spanish Civil War in 1939 when she fell in love with another correspondent, Ernest Hemingway.

Martha and her husband.

The couple moved to Cuba and married, whereupon Hemingway apparently expected Gellhorn to tie on an apron and keep house. Instead, Gellhorn continued traveling to far-off lands to report on conflicts. Hemingway resorted to undermining her career by snagging the sole press credential her employer had issued to cover the D-Day invasion. Not about to be scooped by her husband, Gellhorn talked her way onto a hospital ship and hid in a bathroom overnight. When she emerged, the invasion was underway. The ship she was on was the first hospital ship to arrive, and all hands were desperately needed. Gellhorn fetched food and bandages, water and coffee, and helped interpret where she could. When night fell, she went ashore at Omaha Beach with the medics, not as a journalist, but as a litter-bearer to recover the wounded, flinging herself into the icy surf behind the minesweepers. Gellhorn was the only member of the press to have been near the battle; Hemingway and the rest had watched through binoculars from a safe distance. Hemingway's coverage received far more attention, but the truth had been written—there were 160,000 men on that beach—and one woman. Gellhorn and Hemingway divorced less than a year later, and Gellhorn continued covering wars into her eighties.

AFTERWORD

•

Mark Twain said, "Get your facts first, then you can distort them as you please." The difference between facts and what we do with them is a pervasive concept throughout all human endeavors. Facts, depending on how they are used, are engaging, entertaining, enlightening, disruptive, and dangerous to both the speaker and the spoken to.

Without pontification or hyperbole, facts can be simple. If one holds an apple at shoulder height and releases it, the apple will drop to the ground, no matter who is sitting under it. Whether it is the result of gravity or God is where the discussion begins.

When presented accurately, facts are objective and neither inherently popular nor unpopular. One of the most notable aspects of this book is that the author points out that famously "bad" people did some good things and famously "good" people did some bad things, highlighting that leaders rarely appear wearing "angel" or "monster" badges. Facts may set you free, but they can also annoy you.

Facts can also be boring, but not in this book. In reality (or factually), these are "fact stories" which elucidate the facts presented. The author has a wry style of writing that keeps the reader engaged but not depressed, even though facts about quite tragic events are presented. Her choice of topics and method of presenting the facts and moving on allows the reader to consider them and "store up" their ideas for later consideration.

In this book, the words "Let the facts speak for themselves," come to mind. Her views about women in society are addressed by the presentation and elucidation of facts without lecturing. Especially enjoyable is the fact that the author does not employ an, "I have the answer if you will only listen to me" perspective.

I especially recommend the section "The Real Cost of Food" and those that follow, not because I intend to become a vegan or even give up a good steak. In the spirit of respect for the value of facts in and of themselves, the author presents facts about the problems and the facts that bring the assumed solutions into question. It is almost as if she wants us to think for ourselves. Go figure.

This is an enjoyable book to read. After reading it, I will be able to randomly open it to any page and begin reading again with interest. There is one word of caution, however. There can be a difficulty if you find yourself reading the book while sitting next to someone, be they friend, partner, or even innocent stranger on a subway or plane. Even as they sit quietly reading, texting, etc., you will find yourself saying, excitedly, "Let me just read one fact to you." Of course, you will not be able to read just one.

—Dennis K Kilgore, author of *Time Passes*

ACKNOWLEDGMENTS

•

Accuracy of the facts and precision of language are principally important, so if you have a credible source that refutes a statement you read here, call us at the studio.

With sincere thanks but without a logical order:

Emily Prokop, host of *The Story Behind* podcast and its accompanying book, for connecting me with the great folks at Mango Publishing. It's a huge reward for showing you Boris's new kitten on YouTube.

The amazing people who listen to my podcast. You don't have to let me have a half hour of your time every week, but you do. Thanks especially to whoever the first person was to come across YBOF without knowing me personally and decided to give it a go. The other particularly fabulous listeners are the ones who have been generous enough to give me actually money for prattling into the electronic void.[4] It helped me pay (or at least justify) going to the conference where I shared a hotel room with Emily, thus resulting this book.

My husband, Bobby. You know what you did.

---

4   As of the date of publication: Adam, Amber, Baron, Christina, Cindra, Dan, Darrin, two
     Erics, Jamey, Jean, Jennifer, Kate, Kaylee, Mackenzie, Maria, four Michaels, Ruthann, Ryan,
     Scott, Sean, Seth, Taylor, Troy, and folks calling themselves Crispyplatypus, Cupcake, and
     WhaleBiscuit.

INDEX

●

V

W

X

Y

Z

BIBLIOGRAPHY

•

What's in a (Scientific) Name?:

Frost, Joe. "The Thagomizer: A Stegosaurus' Tail Is Named after a Joke from the '80s." Techly. May 25, 2016. Accessed April 2019. www.techly.com.au/2015/09/22/thagomizer-stegosaurus-tail-named-joke-80s.

Isaak, Mark. "Etymology: Named after People." Curiosities of Biological Nomenclature. Accessed April 2019. www.curioustaxonomy.net/etym/people.html.

Jinkinson, Bethan. "10 Species Named after Famous People." BBC News. July 19, 2012. Accessed April 2019. www.bbc.com/news/magazine-18889495.

Welsh, Jennifer. "StarStruck: Species Named after Celebrities." LiveScience. January 13, 2012. Accessed April 2019. www.livescience.com/17910-species-named-celebrities.html.

Worboys, Audrey. "18 Famous People Who Actually Have an Entire Species Named after Them." BuzzFeed. March 24, 2019. Accessed April 2019. www.buzzfeed.com/audreyworboys/animals-scientifically-named-after-celebrities.

Yanega, Doug. "Curious Scientific Names." University of California Riverside. April 15, 2012. Accessed April 2019. cache.ucr.edu/~heraty/yanega.html#Curious Scientific Names.

Love Hurts:

Andrew, Elise. "Flatworm Mating: Literally a Cockblock." IFLScience. March 11, 2019. Accessed May 07, 2019. www.iflscience.com/plants-and-animals/flatworm-mating-literally-cockblock/.

Banana Slug. Accessed May 07, 2019. kennethadair.org/banana.htm.

Carey, Bjorn. "The Painful Realities of Hyena Sex." LiveScience. April 26, 2006. Accessed May 07, 2019. www.livescience.com/699-painful-realities-hyena-sex.html.

"Green Spoon Worm—Facts, Habitat, Diet and Information." Animal Facts. Accessed May 07, 2019. animalfactsbit.blogspot.com/2017/04/green-spoon-worm-facts-habitat-diet-and.html.

Holekamp, Kay E. "How Spotted Hyenas Mate." *The New York Times*. July 19, 2011. Accessed May 07, 2019. scientistatwork.blogs.nytimes.com/2011/07/19/how-spotted-hyenas-mate/.

Holekamp, Kay E. "Male or Female? Good Question!" *The New York Times*. June 29, 2011. Accessed May 07, 2019. scientistatwork.blogs.nytimes.com/2011/06/29/male-or-female-good-question/.

Keartes, Sarah. "Sex Changes, Sperm Slaves & Ballooning Bodies: Spoon Worms Are Really Weird." Earth Touch News Network. February 14, 2018. Accessed May 07, 2019. www.earthtouchnews.com/natural-world/animal-behaviour/sex-changes-sperm-slaves-ballooning-bodies-spoon-worms-are-really-weird.

MinuteEarth. "Why Do Female Hyenas Have Pseudo-Penises?!" YouTube. October 04, 2017. Accessed May 07, 2019. www.youtube.com/watch?v=-Egtbs-go4Q.

MinuteEarth. "Why It Sucks to Be a Male Hyena." YouTube. July 19, 2017. Accessed May 07, 2019. www.youtube.com/watch?v=PBCNWmU5apE.

Soniak, Matt. "The Horrors of Anglerfish Mating." Mental Floss. July 22, 2014. Accessed May 07, 2019. mentalfloss.com/article/57800/horrors-anglerfish-mating.

"The Largest Penis in The Animal Kingdom." *National Geographic*. April 21, 2016. Accessed May 07, 2019. www.nationalgeographic.com.au/animals/the-largest-penis-in-the-animal-kingdom.aspx.

Woods, James B. "Argonauta Nodosa, Paper Nautilus." Argonauta Nodosa, Paper Nautilus—The Cephalopod Page. Accessed May 07, 2019. www.thecephalopodpage.org/Argo.php.

Yong, Ed. "Scientists Solve Millennia-old Mystery about the Argonaut Octopus." Not Exactly Rocket Science. May 18, 2010. Accessed May 07, 2019. blogs.discovermagazine.com/notrocketscience/2010/05/18/the-argonaut-an-octopus-that-creates-its-own-ballast-tank/#.XNCijBRKgnQ.

Yong, Ed. "In This Insect, Females Have Penises and Males Have Vaginas." *National Geographic*. April 17, 2014. Accessed May 07, 2019. www.nationalgeographic.com/science/phenomena/2014/04/17/in-this-insect-females-have-penises-and-males-have-vaginas/.

Physician, Test Thyself:

Collins, Nick. "Nobel Prizes: Winners Who Experimented on Themselves." *The Telegraph*. October 07, 2013. Accessed May 2019. www.telegraph.co.uk/news/science/science-news/10360202/Nobel-Prizes-Winners-who-experimented-on-themselves.html.

Garrison, Laura Turner. "10 Scientists Who Experimented on Themselves." Mental Floss. November 12, 2011. Accessed May 2019. mentalfloss.com/article/29241/10-scientists-who-experimented-themselves.

Harris, Eleanor. "Eight Scientists Who Became Their Own Guinea Pigs." New Scientist. Accessed May 2019. www.newscientist.com/article/dn16735-eight-scientists-who-became-their-own-guinea-pigs/.

Inglis-Arkell, Esther, and Esther Inglis-Arkell. "Pressure on the Testicle Creates Bizarre Phenomenon of 'Referred Pain.'" Io9. December 16, 2015. Accessed May 2019. io9.gizmodo.com/pressure-on-the-testicle-creates-bizarre-phenomenon-of-1601599162.

Pamo, OG. "Daniel Carrion's Experiment: The Use of Self-infection in the Advance of Medicine." Daniel Carrion's Experiment: The Use of Self-infection in the Advance of Medicine | Royal College of Physicians of Edinburgh.

2012. Accessed May 2019. www.rcpe.ac.uk/college/journal/daniel-carrions-experiment-use-self-infection-advance-medicine.

Pearson, Jordan. "Meet the Scientist Who Injected Himself with 3.5 Million-Year-Old Bacteria." Vice. December 09, 2015. Accessed May 2019. motherboard.vice.com/en_us/article/yp3gg7/meet-the-scientist-who-injected-himself-with-35-million-year-old-bacteria.

Ronson, Jacqueline. "6 Times Self-Experimentation Worked Out despite Being Wildly Dangerous." Inverse. Accessed May 2019. www.inverse.com/article/10480-6-scientists-who-made-great-discoveries-experimenting-on-themselves.

Scharping, Nathaniel. "The Boldest Ideas Scientists Tested on Themselves—D-brief." D. October 31, 2017. Accessed May 2019. blogs.discovermagazine.com/d-brief/2017/10/31/scientists-tested-on-themselves/#.XE0TjuhKjIU.

Taylor, Christie. "From 'Nettles' to 'Volcano,' a Pain Scale for Insect Stings." Science Friday. June 24, 2016. Accessed May 2019. www.sciencefriday.com/segments/from-nettles-to-volcano-a-pain-scale-for-insect-stings/.

"Top 10 Scientists Killed or Injured by Their Experiments." Listverse. June 13, 2014. Accessed May 2019. listverse.com/2008/06/04/top-10-scientists-killed-or-injured-by-their-experiments/.

Unsung-est Heroes:

"About Dr. Hilleman." About Dr. Hilleman | Hilleman Film. October 05, 2018. Accessed April 2019. hillemanfilm.com/dr-hilleman.

C., Anna. "What's in a Name? Frances Oldham Kelsey and the Power of Skepticism." Planned Parenthood Advocates of Arizona. March 08, 2018. Accessed April 2019. advocatesaz.org/2018/03/14/whats-in-a-name-frances-oldham-kelsey-and-the-power-of-skepticism.

"Changing the Face of Medicine | Frances Kathleen Oldham Kelsey." US National Library of Medicine. June 03, 2015. Accessed April 2019. cfmedicine.nlm.nih.gov/physicians/biography_182.html.

"Chinese Nobel Prize Winner Tu Youyou's Drug Has Saved Lives of Millions of Malaria Sufferers." *South China Morning Post*. October 06, 2015. Accessed April 2019. www.scmp.com/news/china/society/article/1864597/drug-chinas-nobel-prize-winner-tu-youyou-worked-has-saved.

Conniff, Richard. "A Forgotten Pioneer of Vaccines." *The New York Times*. May 06, 2013. Accessed April 2019. www.nytimes.com/2013/05/07/health/maurice-hilleman-mmr-vaccines-forgotten-hero.html.

Escobar, Natalie. "You Should Thank Maurice Hilleman for Helping You Live Past the Age of 10." Smithsonian.com. Accessed April 2019. www.smithsonianmag.com/smithsonian-institution/you-should-thank-maurice-hilleman-helping-you-live-past-age-10-180965369/.

Harris, Michele. "The Legacy of Dr. Maurice Hilleman." Erickson Living. June 29, 2018. Accessed April 2019. www.ericksonliving.com/tribune/articles/2018/06/legacy-dr-maurice-hilleman.

"Nobel Journeys: Tu Youyou." EF Tours Blog. February 08, 2018. Accessed July 2019. blog.eftours.com/ef/news/nobel-journeys-tu-youyou.

Reedy, Christianna. "Meet the Woman Who Saved Millions of Lives and Stopped an Epidemic." Futurism. May 16, 2017. Accessed April 2019. futurism.com/meet-the-woman-who-saved-millions-of-lives-and-stopped-an-epidemic.

Su, Xin-Zhuan, and Louis H. Miller. "The Discovery of Artemisinin and the Nobel Prize in Physiology or Medicine." Science China. Life Sciences. November 2015. Accessed April 2019. www.ncbi.nlm.nih.gov/pmc/articles/PMC4966551.

Surprise Polyglot:

"A Brief History of Polari, Gay England's Once-Secret Lingo." Mental Floss. December 01, 2016. Accessed April 2019. mentalfloss.com/article/89393/brief-history-polari-gay-englands-once-secret-lingo.

Alderman, Tim. "Polar Glossary." Timalderman. Accessed April 2019. timalderman.com/tag/polari-glossary.

Bruchac, Marge. "Reclaiming the Word "Squaw" in the Name of the Ancestors." Reclaiming the Word 'Squaw.' " Accessed April 2019. www. nativeweb.org/pages/legal/squaw.html.

Goddard, Ives, and Ives. "Since the Word Squaw Continues to Be of Interest." DSpace Home. April 15, 1997. Accessed April 2019. repository.si.edu/ handle/10088/94999.

Greene, Jordan. "List Monday—Yiddish Words for Penis." Hootings & Howlings. January 06, 2016. Accessed April 2019. airjordang.wordpress. com/2014/04/06/list-monday-yiddish-words-for-penis.

"History of English." EnglishClub. Accessed April 2019. www.englishclub. com/history-of-english.

Kemmer, Suzanne. "Loanwords." Words in English: Loanwords. Accessed April 2019. www.ruf.rice.edu/~kemmer/Words/loanwords.html.

"Loanwords: What Are They and Where Do They Come From?" London Translations. March 10, 2017. Accessed April 2019. www.londontranslations. co.uk/language-services/what-are-loanwords.

Short, William. "What Does the Word Viking Mean?" Hurstwic. Accessed April 2019. www.hurstwic.org/history/articles/text/word_viking.htm.

Sitzman, Ryan. "Did You Know Many English Words Come from Other Languages? Here Are 45!" FluentU English. July 03, 2018. Accessed April 2019. www.fluentu.com/blog/english/english-words-from-other-languages.

Steinmetz, Sol. "Yiddish: What You Should Know." My Jewish Learning. October 30, 2003. Accessed April 2019. www.myjewishlearning.com/article/ yiddish-basics.

"The Secret Language of Polari." National Museums Liverpool. Accessed April 2019. www.liverpoolmuseums.org.uk/maritime/visit/floor-plan/life-at-sea/ gaylife/polari.aspx.

"The Yiddish Handbook: 40 Words You Should Know." Daily Writing Tips. Accessed April 2019. www.dailywritingtips.com/the-yiddish-handbook-40-words-you-should-know.

"Yiddish." Judaism 101: Yiddish Language and Culture. Accessed April 2019. www.jewfaq.org/yiddish.htm.

Good Mourning to You:

"Colours of Mourning in Different Cultures of the World." Funeral Guide. October 26, 2017. Accessed April 2019. www.funeralzone.com.au/blog/mourning-colours.

Desk, League Culture. "This Rajasthani Tribe Celebrates Death, Mourns Birth." League of India. May 22, 2018. Accessed April 2019. leagueofindia.com/culture-heritage/rajasthani-tribe-celebrates-death-mourns-birth.

"Funeral & Burial Rituals from Around the World." Everplans. Accessed April 2019. www.everplans.com/articles/funeral-burial-rituals-from-around-the-world.

Guy-Ryan, Jessie. "The Balinese Cremation Ceremony Admired by David Bowie." Atlas Obscura. January 31, 2016. Accessed April 2019. www.atlasobscura.com/articles/the-balinese-cremation-ceremony-admired-by-bowie.

KidSpirit. "Mourning Around the World." The Huffington Post. December 07, 2017. Accessed April 2019. www.huffingtonpost.com/kidspirit/mourning-around-the-world_b_1542935.html.

Lichtefeld, Chandler. "Grief: Ritual Finger Amputaion." Anthropological Perspectives on Death. February 24, 2017. Accessed April 2019. scholarblogs.emory.edu/gravematters/2017/02/24/grief-ritual-finger-amputaion.

Marinasohma. "Sky Burial: Tibet's Ancient Tradition for Honoring the Dead." Ancient Origins. November 15, 2016. Accessed April 2019. www.ancient-origins.net/history-ancient-traditions/sky-burial-tibet-s-ancient-tradition-honoring-dead-007016.

May, Kate Torgovnick. "Death Is Not the End: Fascinating Funeral Traditions from Around the Globe." Ideas.ted.com. January 04, 2016. Accessed April 2019. ideas.ted.com/11-fascinating-funeral-traditions-from-around-the-globe.

Mumbai, Bachi Karkaria in. "Death in the City: How a Lack of Vultures Threatens Mumbai's 'Towers of Silence.'" *The Guardian*. January 26, 2015. Accessed April 2019. www.theguardian.com/cities/2015/jan/26/death-city-lack-vultures-threatens-mumbai-towers-of-silence.

Munnik, Jo, and Katy Scott. "Famadihana: The Family Reunion Where the Dead Get an Invite." CNN. March 28, 2017. Accessed April 2019. www.cnn.com/2016/10/18/travel/madagascar-turning-bones/index.html.

Ohno, Nuzo. "6 Beautiful African Death Rituals." Female First. October 03, 2017. Accessed April 2019. www.femalefirst.co.uk/books/nuzo-onoh-dead-corpse-1095720.html.

Sakakeeny, Matt. "Jazz Funerals and Second Line Parades." 64 Parishes. Accessed April 2019. 64parishes.org/entry/jazz-funerals-and-second-line-parades.

Thorpe, JR. "How Different Cultures View Death Around the World." Bustle. June 12, 2019. Accessed April 2019. www.bustle.com/articles/97030-5-interesting-death-and-funeral-rituals-around-the-world-from-mongolia-to-sweden.

"Zoroastrian Towers of Silence." Atlas Obscura. October 11, 2013. Accessed April 2019. www.atlasobscura.com/places/zoroastrian-towers-of-silence.

Baptism By...

"10 of the Most Bizarre Baptisms." Listverse. April 14, 2018. Accessed April 2019. listverse.com/2018/04/17/10-of-the-most-bizarre-baptisms.

Babatunde, Mark. "7 Most Fascinating Traditional African Baby Naming Ceremonies." Face2Face Africa. October 16, 2016. Accessed April 2019.

face2faceafrica.com/article/7-fascinating-traditional-african-baby-naming-ceremonies/4.

Burke, Daniel. "Why Do Mormons Baptize the Dead?" *The Washington Post.* Accessed April 2019. www.washingtonpost.com/national/on-faith/why-do-mormons-baptize-the-dead/2012/02/15/gIQAnYfOGR_story.html?utm_term=.5dd60fa91938.

Clark, Amy Sara. "Another Newborn Herpes Case Tied to Metzitzah in NY." *Jewish Week.* Accessed April 2019. jewishweek.timesofisrael.com/another-newborn-herpes-case-tied-to-metzitzah.

Criss, Doug. "Mormons Don't Want You Calling Them Mormons Anymore." CNN. August 17, 2018. Accessed April 2019. www.cnn.com/2018/08/17/us/mormon-church-name-trnd/index.html.

Gilgoff, Dan. "Explainer: How and Why Do Mormons Baptize the Dead?" CNN. February 16, 2012. Accessed April 2019. religion.blogs.cnn.com/2012/02/16/explainer-how-and-why-do-mormons-baptize-the-dead.

Jauregui, Andres. "Satanists Hold Protest Against Westboro Church That Must Be Seen to Be Believed." The Huffington Post. December 07, 2017. Accessed April 2019. www.huffingtonpost.com/2013/07/18/pink-mass-westboro-baptist-church-gay-satanists_n_3616642.html.

Mccombs, Brady. "Mormon Baptisms of Holocaust Victims Draw Ire." AP NEWS. December 21, 2017. Accessed April 2019. apnews.com/992dd887f7b948d0a08055dff0363aa4.

"Naming Traditions and Ceremonies from Around the World." Confetti.co.uk. June 04, 2018. Accessed April 2019. www.confetti.co.uk/wedding-advice/relationships/naming-traditions-and-ceremonies-from-around-the-world.

Odeke-Onyango, Julius. "Imbalu: Turning Boys into Men among the Bamasaba." *Daily Monitor.* August 11, 2018. Accessed April 2019. www.monitor.co.ug/Magazines/Life/Imbalu--Turning-boys-into-men-among-the-Bamasaba/689856-4708518-bj1vvyz/index.html.

Smith, Jonathan. "Satanists Turned the Founder of the Westboro Baptist Church's Dead Mom Gay." Vice. July 17, 2013. Accessed April 2019. www.vice.com/en_us/article/5gwnj8/satanists-turned-the-founder-of-the-westboro-baptist-churchs-mom-gay.

Teicher, Jordan. "Here Are 10 Famous People Posthumously Baptized by Mormons." *Business Insider*. March 02, 2012. Accessed April 2019. www.businessinsider.com/here-are-10-people-posthumously-baptized-by-mormons-2012-3#pope-john-paul-ii-8.

Them's Biting Words:

Anderson, Hephzibah. "Culture—Dorothy Parker's Stunning Wit and Tragic Life." BBC. June 07, 2017. Accessed July 2019. www.bbc.com/culture/story/20170605-dorothy-parkers-stunning-wit-and-tragic-life.

Banac, Ivo. "Josip Broz Tito." *Encyclopædia Britannica*. June 07, 2019. Accessed July 2019. www.britannica.com/biography/Josip-Broz-Tito.

Dickson, Sam. "Winston Churchill's Greatest Jokes and Insults." The Vintage News. October 01, 2016. Accessed July 2019. www.thevintagenews.com/2015/08/01/winston-churchills-greatest-jokes-and-insults/.

Dorfman, Lawrence. *The Snark Handbook: Comebacks, Taunts, and Effronteries*. New York, NY: Skyhorse Publishing, 2015.

Fowler, Will. *D-Day: Omaha and Utah (D-Day: The First 24 Hours Book 3)*. Amber Books. June 02, 2014. Accessed July 2019.

Frizzelle, Christopher. "Dorothy Parker Told the Guys She Hung Out with About Her Abortion, But They Didn't Want to Hear It." The Stranger. October 07, 2015. Accessed July 2019. www.thestranger.com/blogs/slog/2015/10/07/22975406/dorothy-parker-told-the-guys-she-hung-out-with-about-her-abortion-but-they-didnt-want-to-hear-it.

Johnson, David E., and Johnny Ray. Johnson. *A Funny Thing Happened on the Way to the White House: Foolhardiness, Folly, and Fraud in Presidential*

Elections from Andrew Jackson to George W. Bush. Lanham, MD: Taylor Trade Pub., 2004.

Laite, Dixie. "Oooh, Snap! Famous Writers Who Can Really Throw Some Shade: Dixie Laite: A Broad's Perspective." A Broad's Perspective. August 15, 2014. Accessed July 2019. www.dixielaite.com/single-post/2014/07/28/ Oooh-Snap-Famous-Writers-Who-Can-Really-Throw-Some-Shade.

Lederer, Richard, Ben Railton, and Troy Brownfield. "Lincoln as Jokester." *The Saturday Evening Post*. June 25, 2013. Accessed July 2019. www. saturdayeveningpost.com/2013/06/lincoln-jokes.

Medvedev, Roj Aleksandrovič, Zhores A. Medvedev, and Ellen Dahrendorf. *The Unknown Stalin: His Life, Death, and Legacy*. Woodstock N.Y.: Overlook Press, 2004.

"Muhammad Ali at 70: Here's 70 Quotes, Facts, Figures and Videos about The Greatest." Joe Sports. Accessed July 2019. www.joe.ie/sport/muhammad-ali-at-70-heres-70-quotes-facts-figures-and-videos-about-the-greatest-31228.

Powers, Brian. Mark Twain Quotations—Insults. Accessed July 2019. www. twainquotes.com/Insults.html.

Powers, Brian. "The Greatest Insults Part II: Mark Twain Was a Huge Jerk: LATG." Languages Around the Globe. June 03, 2019. Accessed July 2019. latg.org/2019/01/12/greatest-insults-mark-twain#.XSC3uRZKgnR.

Price, Steven D. *The Most Low-down, Lousiest, Loathsome Things Ever Said*. Guilford, CT: Lyons Press, 2017.

"Quote of the Day: The Laconic Phrase." Ricochet. Accessed July 2019. ricochet.com/564559/archives/quote-of-the-day-the-laconic-phrase.

Rockwell, Lew. "The Heroic Swiss." LewRockwell.com. Accessed July 2019. www.lewrockwell.com/2002/12/carlo-stagnaro/the-heroic-swiss/.

Seekins, Briggs. "Ranking Muhammad Ali's 10 Greatest Lines of Trash Talk." Bleacher Report. October 03, 2017. Accessed July 2019. bleacherreport.com/ articles/2645884-ranking-muhammad-alis-10-greatest-lines-of-trash-talk.

Taylor, Rupert. "The Art of the Grand Insult." Owlcation. April 26, 2019. Accessed July 2019. owlcation.com/humanities/The-Art-of-the-Grand-Insult.

"The 23 Most Crushing Insults from All of History." Cracked.com. January 12, 2015. Accessed July 2019. www.cracked.com/pictofacts-243-the-23-most-crushing-insults-from-all-history/.

"The Story of Leonidas and the Legendary Battle of the 300 at Thermopylae." Athens Insiders. Accessed July 2019. athensinsiders.com/the-story-of-leonidas-and-the-legendary-battle-of-the-300-at-thermopylae/.

Walter, Liza. "19 Quotes from All-American (& TOTALLY Sassy) Author, Dorothy Parker." YourTango. August 24, 2016. Accessed July 2019. www.yourtango.com/2016294214/dorothy-parker-quotes-sassy-strong-woman.

Whiteman, Hilary. " 'Sting like a Bee': Best Quotes from Muhammad Ali." CNN. June 04, 2016. Accessed July 2019. www.cnn.com/2016/06/04/sport/best-quotes-muhammad-ali/index.html.

Fighting Girlfriend and the Night Witches:

Dowdy, Linda. "The Night Witches." Aviation—The Night Witches. Accessed June 2019. www.seizethesky.com/nwitches/nitewtch.html.

Holland, Brynn. "Meet the Night Witches, the Daring Female Pilots Who Bombed Nazis By Night." History.com. July 07, 2017. Accessed June 2019. www.history.com/news/meet-the-night-witches-the-daring-female-pilots-who-bombed-nazis-by-night.

Naughton, Russell. "Soviet Women Pilots." Monash University. Accessed June 2019. www.ctie.monash.edu.au/hargrave/soviet_women_pilots.html.

Porath, Jason. "Mariya Oktyabrskaya: The Tank-Driving Widow." Rejected Princesses. Accessed June 2019. www.rejectedprincesses.com/princesses/mariya-oktyabrskaya.

Russell, Shahan. "Nazis Killed Her Husband, She Bought and Drove a T-34 & Then Went on a Rampage." WAR HISTORY ONLINE. November 14, 2017. Accessed June 2019. www.warhistoryonline.com/world-war-ii/

amazing-nazis-killed-her-husband-she-bought-drove-a-t34-then-went-on-a-rampage-m.html.

Mixed Bags of History:

"10 Amazingly Good Acts Performed by Bad People." Listverse. June 24, 2015. Accessed April 2019. listverse.com/2015/06/27/10-amazingly-good-acts-performed-by-bad-people.

"10 Inspiring Tales of Evil Groups Unexpectedly Doing Good." Listverse. January 18, 2019. Accessed April 2019. listverse.com/2015/07/04/10-inspiring-tales-of-evil-groups-unexpectedly-doing-good.

"10 People Who Did Terrible Things for Good Reasons." Toptenz.net. March 08, 2016. Accessed April 2019. www.toptenz.net/10-people-who-did-terrible-things-for-good-reasons.php.

"16 Horrible People Who Did Surprisingly Good Things Once in Their Lives." Storypick. February 22, 2016. Accessed April 2019. www.storypick.com/bad-people-good-things.

"Al Capone's Soup Kitchen during the Great Depression, 1931." Rare Historical Photos. October 14, 2017. Accessed April 2019. rarehistoricalphotos.com/al-capones-soup-kitchen-great-depression-chicago-1931.

All Day. "9 Famous Anti-Semitic People." YouTube. February 11, 2015. Accessed April 2019. www.youtube.com/watch?v=eTVXFQ-S6eA&t=44s.

Austin, Ethan. "Four Things I Learned Visiting a Neighborhood Pablo Escobar Helped Create." Medium. May 26, 2016. Accessed April 2019. medium.com/startupsandburritos/four-things-i-learned-visiting-a-neighborhood-pablo-escobar-helped-create-dfda3d9d9c82.

Barnes, Angie. "20 Beloved Historical Figures Who Did Truly Terrible Things." Boredom Therapy. Accessed April 2019. boredomtherapy.com/historical-figures-questionable-pasts.

Brown, DeNeen L. "When Portland Banned Blacks: Oregon's Shameful History as an 'all-white' State." *The Washington Post*. June 07, 2017. Accessed April 2019. www.washingtonpost.com/news/retropolis/wp/2017/06/07/when-portland-banned-blacks-oregons-shameful-history-as-an-all-white-state.

Frey, Zachary. "6 Historical Heroes Who Did Awful Things Nobody Talks About." Cracked.com. July 21, 2015. Accessed April 2019. www.cracked.com/article_22704_6-historical-heroes-who-did-awful-things-nobody-talks-about.html.

"Genghis Khan: Barbarian or Hero?" Horseback Mongolia. January 05, 2016. Accessed April 2019. www.mongolia-trips.com/genghis-khan-barbarian-or-hero.

Gewen, Barry. "Abraham Lincoln, Racist." *The New York Times*. December 10, 2008. Accessed April 2019. artsbeat.blogs.nytimes.com/2008/12/10/abraham-lincoln-racist.

Hornshaw, Phil, and Ross A. Lincoln. "No, 'Black Panther' Was Not Named After the Black Panther Party." TheWrap. February 20, 2018. Accessed April 2019. www.thewrap.com/black-panther-name-black-panther-party.

James, David. "Napoleon: Hero or Tyrant?" Social Learning. January 13, 2017. Accessed April 2019. sociallearningcommunity.com/napoleon-hero-or-tyrant.

Light, Alan. "Ballad of the 13-Year-Old Bride." Medium. May 01, 2017. Accessed April 2019. medium.com/cuepoint/ballad-of-the-13-year-old-bride-f909cbe1c6b4.

Oliver, Mark. "24 Musicians Whose Legacies Could Face A #MeToo Reckoning." All That's Interesting. November 08, 2018. Accessed April 2019. allthatsinteresting.com/rock-stars-sexual-misconduct#8.

Peterson, Jessie. "Why Don't We Talk About Chuck Berry's Dark Past?" TrackRecord. January 31, 2018. Accessed April 2019. trackrecord.net/why-dont-we-talk-about-chuck-berrys-dark-past-1818518508.

Tharoor, Shashi. "The Ugly Briton." *Time*. November 29, 2010. Accessed April 2019. content.time.com/time/magazine/article/0,9171,2031992,00.html.

"The Bengali Famine." The International Churchill Society. October 24, 2017. Accessed April 2019. winstonchurchill.org/resources/in-the-media/churchill-in-the-news/bengali-famine.

Wenham, Kitty. "Mother Teresa's Sainthood Is a Fraud, Just Like She Was." Medium. September 07, 2016. Accessed April 2019. medium.com/@KittyWenham/mother-teresas-sainthood-is-a-fraud-just-like-she-was-eb395177572.

Workneh, Lilly, and Taryn Finley. "27 Important Facts Everyone Should Know About the Black Panthers." The Huffington Post. February 19, 2018. Accessed April 2019. www.huffingtonpost.com/entry/27-important-facts-everyone-should-know-about-the-black-panthers_us_56c4d853e4b08ffac1276462.

Read a Rainbow:

Andrews, Evan. "The Green Book: The Black Travelers' Guide to Jim Crow America." History.com. February 06, 2017. Accessed April 2019. www.history.com/news/the-green-book-the-black-travelers-guide-to-jim-crow-america.

Bazzi, Mohamad. "What Did Qaddafi's Green Book Really Say?" *The New York Times*. May 27, 2011. Accessed April 2019. www.nytimes.com/2011/05/29/books/review/what-did-qaddafis-green-book-really-say.html.

Cathcart, Adam. "Explainer: What Is Mao's Little Red Book and Why Is Everyone Talking about It?" The Conversation. September 18, 2018. Accessed April 2019. theconversation.com/explainer-what-is-maos-little-red-book-and-why-is-everyone-talking-about-it-51330.

"Commemorating 75 Years of Little Golden Books." PublishersWeekly.com. Accessed April 2019. www.publishersweekly.com/pw/by-topic/childrens/childrens-industry-news/article/72829-commemorating-75-years-of-little-golden-books.html#.

Gale, Thomas. "Little Red Book." *International Encyclopedia of the Social Sciences*. 2008. Accessed April 2019. www.encyclopedia.com/social-sciences/applied-and-social-sciences-magazines/little-red-book.

Kuta, Sarah. "Here's a Look at the Fascinating History of Little Golden Books." Simplemost. July 01, 2019. Accessed April 2019. www.simplemost.com/fascinating-history-little-golden-books.

Nikalos, Katarina. "Qaddafi's Green Book Consigned to the Dustbin of History." Digital Journal: A Global Digital Media Network. September 16, 2011. Accessed April 2019. www.digitaljournal.com/article/311572.

Paster, Pablo. "Ask Pablo: What Is the Impact of All Those Unwanted Phone Books?" TreeHugger. October 11, 2018. Accessed April 2019. www.treehugger.com/culture/ask-pablo-what-is-the-impact-of-all-those-unwanted-phone-books.html.

Stewart, Graham. "When the BBC Banned Baskets and Fig Leaves." *The Times*. November 01, 2008. Accessed April 2019. www.thetimes.co.uk/article/when-the-bbc-banned-baskets-and-fig-leaves-0vbr3q5crnk.

"What's in Gadhafi's Manifesto?" NPR. March 03, 2011. Accessed April 2019. www.npr.org/2011/03/03/134239733/Whats-In-Gadhafis-Manifesto.

"Who, What, Why: What Is the Little Red Book?" BBC News. November 26, 2015. Accessed April 2019. www.bbc.com/news/magazine-34932800.

Yu, Dennis. "Facts You Probably Didn't Know about the Yellow Pages—Dennis Yu: Digital Marketer: Speaker: Agency Builder." Dennis Yu: Digital Marketer | Speaker | Agency Builder. May 07, 2019. Accessed April 2019. www.dennis-yu.com/facts-you-probably-didnt-know-about-the-yellow-pages.

Zasky, Jason. "The Phone Book: The Book That Everyone Uses but No One Reads." *Failure Magazine*. Accessed April 2019. failuremag.com/article/the-phone-book.

To Boldly Go Where Only White Men Had Gone Before:

Bates, Karen Grigsby. "Octavia Butler: Writing Herself into The Story." NPR. July 10, 2017. Accessed July 2019. www.npr.org/sections/codeswitch/2017/07/10/535879364/octavia-butler-writing-herself-into-the-story.

Capozzi, Justine. "Patternist Seriest." Speculative Fiction. May 9, 2015. Accessed July 2019. speculative.sunygeneseoenglish.org/category/butlerspring2015/patternist.

Esme. "Octavia E. Butler: A Pioneering and Prescient Science-Fiction Legacy." Esme. March 26, 2019. Accessed July 2019. esme.com/single-moms/sons-daughters/octavia-butlers-science-fiction-legacy-pioneering-and-prescient.

Francis, Conseula. *Conversations with Octavia Butler*. Jackson: University Press of Mississippi, 2009.

Giles, Chris. "Afrofuturism: The Genre That Made Black Panther." CNN. February 12, 2018. Accessed July 2019. www.cnn.com/2018/02/12/africa/genre-behind-black-panther-afrofuturism/index.html.

Golden, Jill. "How Octavia Butler Inspired Ava Duvernay, Janelle Monae." *Time*. May 04, 2018. Accessed July 2019. time.com/5225461/octavia-butler-janelle-monae.

Grinberg, Emanuella. "Octavia E. Butler: A Visionary among Futurists." CNN. June 22, 2018. Accessed July 2019. www.cnn.com/2018/06/22/culture/octavia-e-butler/index.html.

"Octavia E. Butler." Biography.com. July 23, 2018. Accessed July 2019. www.biography.com/writer/octavia-e-butler.

Temple, Emiliy. "The Grand Cultural Influence of Octavia Butler." Literary Hub. June 21, 2019. Accessed July 2019. lithub.com/the-grand-cultural-influence-of-octavia-butler.

Tenbarge, Kat. "Why Octavia E. Butler Is Referred to as the Mother of Afrofuturism." Inverse. June 22, 2018. Accessed July 2019. www.inverse. com/article/46330-octavia-e-butler-why-she-s-referred-to-as-the-mother-of-afrofuturism.

Yehoussi, Maweni. "Mark Dery." Black(s) To the Future. Accessed July 2019. blackstothefuture.com/en/mark-dery-14-portrait.

Lights, Curses, Action!

"10 Horror Movies That Were Really Cursed." Flavorwire. April 15, 2019. Accessed July 2019. flavorwire.com/520130/10-horror-movies-that-were-really-cursed.

"25 Fascinating Facts About the Exorcist." Listverse. June 16, 2014. Accessed July 2019. listverse.com/2009/10/30/25-fascinating-facts-about-the-exorcist.

"7 of the Strangest and Unexplainable Film Curses." Cinelinx. April 14, 2011. Accessed July 2019. www.cinelinx.com/movie-news/movie-stuff/investigating-the-notorious-film-curse.

Carroll, Rory. "Hollywood and the Downwinders Still Grapple with Nuclear Fallout." *The Guardian*. June 06, 2015. Accessed July 2019. www.theguardian.com/film/2015/jun/06/downwinders-nuclear-fallout-hollywood-john-wayne.

Castillo, Monica. "Is the 'Poltergeist' Curse Real? Here's the True Story Behind the Classic 1982 Horror Movie." *International Business Times*. May 21, 2015. Accessed July 2019. www.ibtimes.com/poltergeist-curse-real-heres-true-story-behind-classic-1982-horror-movie-1932929.

Colburn, Randall. "The Cursed Hollywood Script That Killed Almost Every Actor Who Read It." Ranker. Accessed July 28, 2019. www.ranker. com/list/atuk-cursed-film-facts/randall-colburn?ref=lzyrltdlstszerg_ rr&pos=2&a=42&ltype=l&l=387066&g=2&li_source=LI&li_ medium=desktop-popular-lists.

Harkins, Danny. "The Insane True Stories Behind 6 Cursed Movies." Cracked. com. August 12, 2008. Accessed July 2019. www.cracked.com/article_16541_ the-insane-true-stories-behind-6-cursed-movies.html.

"Haunted Hollywood: The 10 Most Cursed Movies of All Time." The Occult Museum. January 16, 2017. Accessed July 2019. www.theoccultmuseum.com/ haunted-hollywood-10-cursed-movies-time.

Hyman, Peter, and Peter Hyman. "The Development Hell of a Confederacy of Dunces." Slate Magazine. December 14, 2006. Accessed July 2019. slate. com/news-and-politics/2006/12/the-development-hell-of-a-confederacy-of-dunces.html.

McKendry, David Ian. "Is THE EXORCIST Cursed? Seven Reasons Why Some Think the Film Is Haunted." The 13th Floor. February 27, 2018. Accessed July 2019. www.the13thfloor.tv/2015/12/02/is-the-exorcist-movie-cursed.

Pfeifle, Tess. "The Omen's Curse." Astonishing Legends. August 12, 2018. Accessed July 2019. www.astonishinglegends.com/astonishing-legends/2018/8/12/the-omens-curse.

"Poltergeist Eerily Predicted the Death of Heather O'Rourke." Wicked Horror. May 01, 2018. Accessed July 2019. wickedhorror.com/horror-news/ poltergeist-eerily-predicted-death-heather-orourke.

Schilling, Mary Kaye. "Steven Soderbergh on Quitting Hollywood, Getting the Best Out of J. Lo, and His Love of Girls." Vulture. August 08, 2014. Accessed July 2019. www.vulture.com/2013/01/steven-soderbergh-in-conversation.html.

Taylor, Patrick. "Stories from the Set: The Exorcist." One Room with a View. July 10, 2015. Accessed July 2019. oneroomwithaview.com/2014/02/06/ stories-from-the-set-the-exorcist.

Valjak, Doagoj. "The Conqueror." The Vintage News. March 30, 2019. Accessed July 2019. www.thevintagenews.com/2018/02/19/the-conqueror-film.

Writers, Staff. "Studio Sues Comedian for Failing to Do Movie." *The Spokesman-Review* (Spokane, WA), February 27, 1988, People sec. Accessed July 2019. news.google.com/newspapers?nid=1314&dat=19880227&id=Rbsy AAAAIBAJ&sjid=n-8DAAAAIBAJ&pg=3709,5828449.

Fake a Need and Fill It:

Bernazzani, Sophia. "Women Shave Because of Marketers: How the Industry Created Demand for Women's Razors." HubSpot Blog. Accessed April 2019. blog.hubspot.com/marketing/womens-razors-marketing.

Blakemore, Erin. "When New York Banned Smoking to Save Women's Souls." History.com. October 02, 2017. Accessed April 2019. www.history.com/news/ when-new-york-banned-smoking-to-save-womens-souls.

Cartwright, Frederick F. "Joseph Lister." *Encyclopædia Britannica*. Accessed April 2019. www.britannica.com/biography/Joseph-Lister-Baron-Lister-of-Lyme-Regis.

Chakraborty, Rakhi. "Torches of Freedom: How the World's First PR Campaign Came to Be." YourStory.com. August 06, 2014. Accessed April 2019. yourstory.com/2014/08/torches-of-freedom.

Colleary, Eric. "How Bacon and Eggs Became the American Breakfast." The American Table. May 01, 2013. Accessed April 2019. www.americantable. org/2012/07/how-bacon-and-eggs-became-the-american-breakfast.

Creative, Vox. "The Reason You Love Bacon and Eggs? Science (and Advertising)." Eater. February 16, 2018. Accessed April 2019. www.eater. com/ad/17017276/egg-bacon-breakfast-science-public-relations.

Fenster, Bob. *Duh!: The Stupid History of the Human Race*. Kansas City, MO: Andrews McMeel Pub., 2003.

Komar, Marlen. "The Sneaky History of Why Women Started Shaving." Bustle. June 12, 2019. Accessed April 2019. www.bustle.com/articles/196747- the-sneaky-manipulative-history-of-why-women-started-shaving.

"Listerine." National Museum of American History. Accessed April 2019. americanhistory.si.edu/collections/search/object/nmah_1170944.

Panati, Charles. *Extraordinary Origins of Everyday Things*. New York: Harper & Row, 1989.

Turney, Michael. "Edward Bernays: Father and Philosopher of Public Relations." Edward Bernays. August 15, 2015. Accessed April 2019. www.nku. edu/~turney/prclass/readings/bernays.html.

"Was Halitosis Invented by Listerine?" Vision Times. February 16, 2018. Accessed April 2019. www.visiontimes.com/2018/02/16/was-halitosis-invented-by-listerine.html.

Zhang, Sarah, and Sarah Zhang. "How "Clean" Was Sold to America with Fake Science." Gizmodo. February 13, 2015. Accessed April 2019. gizmodo. com/how-clean-was-sold-to-america-1685320177.

Veteran of the Format Wars:

"8 Facts You Probably Forgot about 8-tracks." MeTV. April 11, 2016. Accessed April 2019. metv.com/lists/8-facts-you-probably-forgot-about-8-tracks.

Biderman, David. "11 Minutes of Action." *The Wall Street Journal*. January 15, 2010. Accessed April 2019. www.wsj.com/articles/SB1000142405274870 4281204575002852055561406.

Demain, Bill. "How Mister Rogers Saved the VCR." Mental Floss. June 07, 2018. Accessed April 2019. mentalfloss.com/article/29686/how-mister-rogers-saved-vcr.

Harris, Robin. "HD DVD Post-mortem: Why Did Toshiba Fail?" ZDNet. February 19, 2008. Accessed April 2019. www.zdnet.com/article/hd-dvd-post-mortem-why-did-toshiba-fail.

"How Laserdisc Ultimately Won the Format Wars." Today I Found Out. September 01, 2016. Accessed April 2019. www.todayifoundout.com/index. php/2016/08/why-Laserdisc-lost.

"How Sony's BetaMax Lost to JVC's VHS." Engineer Guy. June 17, 2014. Accessed April 2019. www.engineerguy.com/failure/betamax.htm.

Lowbrow, Yeoman. "The Eight-Track Miracle: 8 Reasons It Failed." Flashbak. April 23, 2014. Accessed April 2019. flashbak.com/the-eight-track-miracle-8-reasons-it-failed-2034.

"Notice of the End of Shipment of Beta Video Cassette and Micro MV Cassette Tape." Sony Japan. November 10, 2015. Accessed April 2019. www.sony.co.jp/SonyInfo/News/Press/201511/15-1110/index.html.

OddityArchive. "Disposable DVD's (DIVX & Flexplay)." YouTube. April 14, 2016. Accessed April 2019. www.youtube.com/watch?v=V3KIqgLIrsE.

Owen, Dave. "The Betamax vs VHS Format War." May 01, 2005. Accessed April 2019. www.mediacollege.com/video/format/compare/betamax-vhs.html.

"Slower Than Slow: 16 RPM Records." Slower Than Slow: 16 RPM Records. March 12, 2011. Accessed April 2019. bloggerhythms.blogspot.com/2011/05/slower-than-slow-16-rpm-records.html.

"The Ultimate Audio Format War: Records vs. Wax Cylinders." Neatorama. September 30, 2010. Accessed April 2019. www.neatorama.com/2010/09/30/the-ultimate-audio-format-war-records-vs-wax-cylinders.

"Worried About Disc Rot? Here's How to Look After Your CDs: Discogs." Discogs Blog. February 04, 2019. Accessed April 2019. blog.discogs.com/en/say-no-to-disc-rot-how-to-look-after-cds.

Laws of the Internet:

"A Quote from Reaper Man." Goodreads. Accessed July 2019. www.goodreads.com/quotes/51665-five-exclamation-marks-the-sure-sign-of-an-insane-mind.

Ahola, Jussi. "Cunningham's Law and Human Motivation." Medium. June 01, 2014. Accessed July 2019. medium.com/@jussiahola/cunninghams-law-and-human-motivation-d88063fdc098.

"Attempt to Suppress Can Backfire." Today's Business Law. September 27, 2007. Accessed July 2019. archive. is/20070927014240/http://www.lfpress.ca/cgi-bin/publish. cgi?p=111404&x=articles&s=shopping#selection-1541.0-1553.209.

"Big Contradictions in the Evolution Theory." Christian Forums. Accessed July 2019. web.archive.org/web/20170114124412/http:// www.christianforums.com/threads/big-contradictions-in-the-evolution-theory.1962980/page-3#post-17606580.

Binning, Sarah Ann. "Hartman's Law." I Spy Grammar. Accessed July 2019. ispygrammar.wordpress.com/tag/hartmans-law.

Brandolini, Alberto. "The Bullshit Asymmetry: The Amount of Energy Needed to Refute Bullshit Is an Order of Magnitude Bigger than to Produce It." Twitter. January 11, 2013. Accessed July 2019. twitter.com/ziobrando/ status/289635060758507521.

Chivers, Tom. "Internet Rules and Laws: The Top 10, from Godwin to Poe." *The Telegraph*. October 23, 2009. Accessed July 2019. www.telegraph. co.uk/technology/news/6408927/Internet-rules-and-laws-the-top-10-from-Godwin-to-Poe.html.

Dawson, George. "Brandolini's Law." Brandolini's Law. January 01, 2016. Accessed July 2019. real-psychiatry.blogspot.com/2016/12/ brandolinis-law.html.

Dempsey, John, and Dictionary.com. "What Does Lewis's Law Mean?" Dictionary.com. April 12, 2019. Accessed July 2019. www.dictionary.com/e/ pop-culture/lewiss-law.

Godwin, Mike. "Meme, Counter-meme." Wired. December 20, 2017. Accessed July 2019. www.wired.com/1994/10/godwin-if-2.

Greenwood, Max. "Judge Dismisses Defamation Suit from Ex-Sputnik Journalist." The Hill. June 07, 2018. Accessed July 2019. thehill.com/ homenews/media/391108-judge-dismisses-defamation-suit-against-journalist-who-suggested-woman-used.

"Hartman's Law Confirmed Again." Language Log. April 04, 2005. Accessed July 2019. itre.cis.upenn.edu/~myl/languagelog/archives/002035.html.

Mandelbaum, Ryan F. "Godwin of Godwin's Law: 'By All Means, Compare These Shitheads to the Nazis.' " Gizmodo. March 23, 2018. Accessed July 2019. gizmodo.com/godwin-of-godwins-law-by-all-means-compare-these-shi-1797807646.

Marwick, Alice. "Donglegate: Why the Tech Community Hates Feminists." Wired. June 04, 2017. Accessed July 2019. www.wired.com/2013/03/richards-affair-and-misogyny-in-tech.

Ohlheiser, Abby. "Porn, Nazis and Sarcasm: How These 3 Old Rules Basically Explain the Entire Internet." *The Washington Post*. June 23, 2017. Accessed July 2019. www.washingtonpost.com/news/the-intersect/wp/2017/06/23/the-three-old-rules-that-explain-basically-the-entire-internet-in-2017/?utm_term=.79d349e4a5e4.

"Reproduced by Permission of Harry Frankfurt, a Member of the Philosophy Faculty at Princeton University." Harry Frankfurt on Bullshit. Accessed July 2019. web.archive.org/web/20050308024618/http://www.tauroscatology.com/frankfurt.htm.

Robertson, Lori. "That Chain E-mail Your Friend Sent to You Is (Likely) Bogus. Seriously." FactCheck.org. February 15, 2017. Accessed July 2019. www.factcheck.org/2008/03/that-chain-e-mail-your-friend-sent-to-you-is-likely-bogus-seriously.

Schott, Ben. "Weekend Competition: Schott's Law." *The New York Times*. May 28, 2010. Accessed July 2019. schott.blogs.nytimes.com/2010/05/28/weekend-competition-schotts-law/?_php=true&_type=blogs&permid=119&_r=0#comment119.

Shafer, Jack, David Siders, and Anya Van Wagtendonk. "The Limits of Fact-Checking." POLITICO Magazine. December 24, 2015. Accessed July 2019. www.politico.com/magazine/story/2015/12/the-limits-of-the-fact-checker-213461.

"Skitt's Law." A Sycophant of the Bourgeoisie. February 28, 2007. Accessed July 2019. sycophant.wordpress.com/2007/02/28/skitts-law.

"Skitt's Law." Know Your Meme. July 17, 2018. Accessed July 2019. knowyourmeme.com/memes/skitt-s-law.

Solon, Olivia. "From Beyoncé to The Oatmeal: The Streisand Effect at Its Most Glorious." Wired UK. October 04, 2017. Accessed July 2019. www. wired.co.uk/article/streisand-effect.

"THE 'STREISAND EFFECT': THE 5 BIGGEST EXAMPLES!" Globalo. June 26, 2016. Accessed July 2019. www.globalo.com/streisand-effect-5-biggest-examples.

"The Bullshit Asymmetry Principle." Statistical Modeling, Causal Inference, and Social Science:. January 28, 2019. Accessed July 2019. statmodeling.stat. columbia.edu/2019/01/28/bullshit-asymmetry-principle.

"Who Was Cunningham of Cunningham's Law?" "The Best Way to Get the Right Answer on the Internet Is Not to Ask a Question, but to Post the Wrong Answer." Today I Found Out. September 22, 2014. Accessed July 2019. www. todayifoundout.com/index.php/2014/09/cunningham-cunninghams-law.

A World of Pizza:

Filippone, Peggy Trowbridge. "The History of Pizza and How It Became Popular in the US." The Spruce Eats. Accessed May 2019. www.thespruceeats. com/history-of-pizza-1807648.

Stradley, Linda. "Pizza—History and Legends of Pizza." What's Cooking America. October 31, 2016. Accessed May 2019. whatscookingamerica.net/ History/Pizza/PizzaHistory.htm.

Turim, Gayle. "A Slice of History: Pizza Through the Ages." History.com. July 27, 2012. Accessed May 2019. www.history.com/news/a-slice-of-history-pizza-through-the-ages.

What's a Drink Without a Nosh?

Osswald, Gillian. "Hangover Foods from Around the World—Rassol." First We Feast. June 01, 2018. Accessed May 2019. firstwefeast.com/eat/2013/11/hangover-food-from-around-world/rassol.

Ro, Herrine. "The Most Popular Drunk Food in 21 Cities Around the World." *Business Insider*. August 29, 2016. Accessed May 2019. www.businessinsider.com/drunk-foods-around-the-world-2016-8?r=UK&IR=T#sri-lanka-kottu-21.

The Real Cost of Food:

Asmann, Parker. "Powerful Mexico Crime Groups Grew by Extorting Avocado Trade: Report." InSight Crime. November 19, 2017. Accessed May 2019. www.insightcrime.org/news/brief/powerful-mexico-crime-groups-got-their-start-extorting-avocado-trade-report.

Colon, Phil. "Avocado Cartels: The Violent Reality Behind 'Green Gold.'" Inteligencia. August 03, 2018. Accessed May 2019. inteligencia.io/money/avocado-cartels.

Fleischer, Deborah. "Almond Milk Is Taking a Toll on the Environment." UCSF Office of Sustainability. January 2018. Accessed May 2019. sustainability.ucsf.edu/3.713.

Godoy, Emilio. "Migrant Farm Workers, the Main Victims of Slave Labour in Mexico." Inter Press Service. Accessed May 2019. www.ipsnews.net/2019/04/migrant-farm-workers-main-victims-slave-labour-mexico.

Guibourg, Clara, and Helen Briggs. "Climate Change: Which Vegan Milk Is Best?" BBC News. February 22, 2019. Accessed May 2019. www.bbc.com/news/science-environment-46654042.

Howell, Madeleine, and Gareth May. "The Hidden Cruelty of the Cashew Industry—and the Other Fashionable Foods That Aren't as Virtuous as They Appear." *The Telegraph*. December 16, 2015. Accessed May 2019. www.

telegraph.co.uk/food-and-drink/news/healthy-foods-that-are-ruining-the-environment.

"Is Soya Sustainable?" Ethical Consumer. May 10, 2019. Accessed May 2019. www.ethicalconsumer.org/food-drink/soya-sustainable.

Kahn, Carrie. "Blood Avocados No More: Mexican Farm Town Says Its Kicked Out Cartels." NPR. February 02, 2018. Accessed May 2019. www.npr.org/sections/parallels/2018/02/02/582086654/mexicos-avocado-capital-says-it-s-kicked-cartels-off-the-farm.

Larmer, Brook. "How the Avocado Became the Fruit of Global Trade." *The New York Times*. March 27, 2018. Accessed May 2019. www.nytimes.com/2018/03/27/magazine/the-fruit-of-global-trade-in-one-fruit-the-avocado.html.

Lehner, Peter, and Peter Lehner. "The Hidden Costs of Food." HuffPost. August 16, 2017. Accessed May 2019. www.huffpost.com/entry/the-hidden-costs-of-food_b_11492520.

Lewis, Tanya. "The Top 10 Foods with the Biggest Environmental Footprint." *Business Insider*. September 19, 2015. Accessed May 2019. www.businessinsider.com/the-top-10-foods-with-the-biggest-environmental-footprint-2015-9.

"Maps: Global Slavery Index." Maps | Global Slavery Index. 2018. Accessed May 2019. www.globalslaveryindex.org/2018/data/maps/#prevalence.

Nianias, Helen. "Cartels, Kidnapping and Killings: How Avocado Became Problematic." Grazia. Accessed May 2019. graziadaily.co.uk/life/real-life/avocado-became-problematic.

"The Truth About Soy and the Environment." Allplants. Accessed May 2019. allplants.com/blogs/stories/is-the-environmental-impact-of-soy-a-valid-argument-against-a-plant-based-diet.

Young, Richard. "Why Avoiding Meat and Dairy Won't Save the Planet." Climate & Capitalism. June 03, 2018. Accessed May 2019.

climateandcapitalism.com/2018/06/26/why-avoiding-meat-and-dairy-wont-save-the-planet.

Yu, Long. "Superfoods' Dark Side: Increasing Vulnerability of Quinoa Farmers in Bolivia." Global Food Health and Society. Accessed May 2019. web.colby.edu/st297-global18/2019/01/22/superfoods-dark-side-increasing-vulnerability-of-quinoa-farmers-in-bolivia/.

Concave Earthers:

"Edgar Allen Poe, The Narrative of Arthur Gordon Pym." American Studies @ The University of Virginia. Accessed July 2019. xroads.virginia.edu/~MA98/silverman/poe/rey_hist.html.

Foer, Joshua. "Hollow Earth Monument." Atlas Obscura. January 27, 2014. Accessed July 2019. www.atlasobscura.com/places/hollow-Earth-monument.

Grundhauser, Eric. "The Hollow Earth Is Filled with Giants, Germans, and A Little Sun." Atlas Obscura. February 29, 2016. Accessed July 2019. www.atlasobscura.com/articles/the-hollow-Earth-is-filled-with-giants-germans-and-a-little-sun.

"Hollow Earth." Weird Florida. Accessed July 2019. www.weirdus.com/states/florida/fabled_people_and_places/hollow_earth/index.php.

"Hollow Earth Hypothesis—Subterranean Civilizations—Agartha." Crystalinks. Accessed July 2019. www.crystalinks.com/hollowEarth.html.

"Hollow Earth Theory—Subterranean Civilization of Agartha." Gaia. Accessed July 2019. www.gaia.com/article/hollow-earth-theory-is-the-subterranean-civilization-of-agartha-real.

Lamoureux, Mack. "A Journey to the Center of Modern Hollow Earth Theory." Vice. July 18, 2017. Accessed July 2019. www.vice.com/en_us/article/ywgexk/a-journey-to-the-center-of-modern-hollow-earth-theory.

Macdonald, Malcolm. "Search for Hollow Earth." Anderson Valley Advertiser. October 11, 2017. Accessed July 2019. www.theava.com/archives/74194.

Posey, Carl A. The Big Book of Weirdos. Place of Publication Not Identified: Paradox, 1998.

Simanek, Donald E. Turning the Universe Inside-Out. Accessed July 2019. www.lockhaven.edu/~dsimanek/hollow/morrow.htm.

Simon, Matt. "Fantastically Wrong: The Legendary Scientist Who Swore Our Planet Is Hollow." Wired. July 19, 2018. Accessed July 2019. www.wired.com/2014/07/fantastically-wrong-hollow-earth.

Simon, Matt. "Fantastically Wrong: The Legendary Scientist Who Swore Our Planet Is Hollow." Wired. July 19, 2018. Accessed July 2019. www.wired.com/2014/07/fantastically-wrong-hollow-earth.

Ugc. "Koreshan State Historic Site." Atlas Obscura. September 13, 2016. Accessed July 2019. www.atlasobscura.com/places/koreshan-state-historic-site.

Vanderper, David. "The Hollow Earth in Science." Academia.edu. Accessed July 2019. www.academia.edu/11671577/The_Hollow_Earth_in_Science.

And the Little Child Shall Lead Them:

"10-year-old Turkish Girl Talya Özdemir Becomes Youngest Person Ever to Address the UN." DailySabah. February 11, 2017. Accessed July 2019. www.dailysabah.com/science/2017/02/11/10-year-old-turkish-girl-talya-ozdemir-becomes-youngest-person-ever-to-address-the-un.

"2019 Iqbal Masih Award for the Elimination of Child Labor." US Department of Labor. Accessed July 2019. www.dol.gov/agencies/ilab/issues/child-labor/iqbal.

"Cris Kesz Valdez." TheXtraordinary. Accessed July 2019. www.thextraordinary.org/cris-kesz-valdez#biography.

Kent, Melissa. "Canadian Teen Tells UN to 'Warrior Up,' Give Water Same Protections as People." CBCnews. March 23, 2018. Accessed July 2019. www.cbc.ca/news/canada/autumn-peltier-un-water-activist-united-nations-1.4584871.

Kuklin, Susan. *Iqbal Masih and the Crusaders against Child Slavery*. New York: H. Holt and, 1998.

"Looking Black on Today in 2001, Nkosi Johnson, The Child Who Changed Public Perceptions of HIV/AIDS Died at Age 12." Black Then. June 02, 2016. Accessed July 2019. blackthen.com/looking-black-on-today-in-2001-nkosi-johnson-the-child-who-changed-public-perceptions-of-hivaids-died-at-age-12.

Medina, Sarah. "Homeless 13-Year-Old Wins $130,000 Children's Peace Prize." HuffPost. September 26, 2012. Accessed July 2019. www.huffpost.com/entry/kesz-valdez_n_1910737.

"Nkosi Johnson's History." Nkosi's Haven. Accessed July 2019. nkosishaven.org/nkosi-johnsons-history.

"Nkosi's Speech." SABC. Accessed July 2019.

"Poverty in the Philippines." Asian Development Bank. May 06, 2019. Accessed July 2019. www.adb.org/countries/philippines/poverty.

Press, The Associated. "Child Labor Critic Is Slain in Pakistan." *The New York Times*. April 19, 1995. Accessed July 2019. www.nytimes.com/1995/04/19/world/child-labor-critic-is-slain-in-pakistan.html.

Rosenberg, Jennifer. "Biography of Iqbal Masih." ThoughtCo. May 25, 2019. Accessed July 2019. www.thoughtco.com/10-year-old-activist-iqbal-masih-1779425.

Ryan, Timothy. "Iqbal Masih's Life—a Call to Human Rights Vigilance." *The Christian Science Monitor*. May 03, 1995. Accessed July 2019. www.csmonitor.com/1995/0503/03181.html.

Soo, Zen. "How a 14-Year-Old HongKonger Built an App for Alzheimer's Patients." *South China Morning Post*. January 30, 2019. Accessed July 2019. www.scmp.com/tech/apps-social/article/2183948/how-14-year-old-hongkonger-built-app-help-alzheimers-patients.

"Street Children Need to Be Healthy, to Be Able to Make Their Dreams Come True." KidsRights. Accessed July 2019. kidsrights.org/Kesz-Valdez.

"Teen Activist Autumn Peltier Who Scolded Trudeau to Address UN." BBC News. December 31, 2017. Accessed July 2019. www.bbc.com/news/world-us-canada-42358227.

Swiss Army Wife:

"3 Ways Marcia Lucas Saved Star Wars." SYFY UK. Accessed May 2019. www.syfy.co.uk/news/3-ways-which-marcia-lucas-helped-save-star-wars-0.

Cellania, Miss. "The Extraordinary Life of Martha Gellhorn, the Woman Ernest Hemingway Tried to Erase." Neatorama. July 18, 2018. Accessed May 2019. www.neatorama.com/2018/07/16/The-Extraordinary-Life-of-Martha-Gellhorn-the-Woman-Ernest-Hemingway-Tried-to-Erase.

Diu, Nisha Lilia. "Mrs Alfred Hitchcock: 'The Unsung Partner.'" The Telegraph. February 08, 2013. Accessed May 2019. www.telegraph.co.uk/culture/film/film-news/9832084/Mrs-Alfred-Hitchcock-The-Unsung-Partner.html.

Ingraham, Christopher. "When Women Inherit Their Husbands' Congressional Seats." *The Washington Post*. March 18, 2014. Accessed May 2019. www.washingtonpost.com/news/wonk/wp/2014/03/18/when-women-inherit-their-husbands-congressional-seats/?utm_term=.4d6905d7cc4c.

"Jeanne De Clisson Biography." Jeanne De Clisson Pirate—Biography and Facts. Accessed May 2019. www.annebonnypirate.com/famous-female-pirates/jeanne-de-clisson.

"Mary Patten, 19 and Pregnant, Takes Command of a Clipper Ship in 1856." New England Historical Society. March 12, 2019. Accessed May 2019. www.newenglandhistoricalsociety.com/mary-patten-19-pregnant-commands-clipper-ship-1856.

Porath, Jason. "Janequeo: The Rebel Spain Never Caught." Rejected Princesses. Accessed May 2019. www.rejectedprincesses.com/princesses/janequeo.

Porath, Jason. "Jeanne De Clisson: The Lioness of Brittany." Rejected Princesses. Accessed May 2019. www.rejectedprincesses.com/princesses/jeanne-de-clisson.

RocketJump. "How Star Wars Was Saved in the Edit." YouTube. December 07, 2017. Accessed May 2019. www.youtube.com/watch?v=GFMyMxMYDNk.

Zar, Dr. "The First Lady Who Secretly Ran the U.S. Government." History and Headlines. October 2, 2013. Accessed May 2019. www.historyandheadlines.com/first-lady-secretly-ran-u-s-government.

Various:

Lewis, Dan. *Now I Know: The Revealing Stories Behind the World's Most Interesting Facts*. Avon, MA: Adams Media Corporation, 2013.

Panati, Charles. *Panatis Browsers Book of Beginnings*. Boston: Houghton Mifflin, 1994.

Weir, William. *History's Greatest Lies: The Startling Truths Behind World Events Our History Books Got Wrong*. Beverly, MA: Fair Winds Press, 2009.

Zacks, Richard. *An Underground Education: The Unauthorized and Outrageous Supplement to Everything You Thought You Knew About Art, Sex, Business, Crime, Science, Medicine, and Other Fields of Human Knowledge*. New York: Anchor Books, 1999.

Zacks, Richard. *History Laid Bare: Love, Sex, and Perversity from the Ancient Etruscans to Warren G. Harding*. New York: HarperPerennial, 1995.

ABOUT THE AUTHOR

•

Growing up with six sisters was guaranteed to have lasting effects, as would attention-deficit/hyperactivity. For Moxie LaBouche, these manifested as an intense appetite for new information and a relentless desire for attention, especially to be the center thereof. For the better part a decade, Moxie performed as a burlesque dancer with a style that ranged from sensual to screwball. She specializes in "nerd-lesque," dressing up as (then undressing as) beloved fictional characters, from "Hot Lips" Houlihan to Eeyore. Regardless of the act, Moxie always had bonus facts for the emcee to include in the introduction. In her burlesque career, Moxie also produced the only George R.R. Martin-approved Game of Thrones tribute show and was invited to speak about burlesque in the 2016 TEDxRVA.

One thing that was consistent throughout Moxie's life was a love of interesting facts. Her brain was filled to overflowing...and overflow it did. Consciously,

Moxie knew that her customers at the grocery store didn't want to hear about the prehistoric ground sloths that used to spread avocado pits (that's why the pits are so huge); they just wanted to pay for their avocados and leave. Still, Moxie could not help herself, even dropping facts into arguments and other awkward social situations.

When the Universe made it clear to Moxie repeatedly that it was time to stop doing burlesque, her husband introduced her to podcasts to help fill the gap. After some reluctance, she tested the waters with *Unorthodox* and *99% Invisible*, and Moxie was hooked. Soon she was subscribed to a hundred shows. The influx of facts in meant that they would have to come out somewhere, so the natural choice was the launch the Your Brain on Facts podcast.

Moxie lives in Virginia with her husband and a dozen or so pets on the property where she used to raise goats and sell handmade soap for a living.

Mango Publishing, established in 2014, publishes an eclectic list of books by diverse authors—both new and established voices—on topics ranging from business, personal growth, women's empowerment, LGBTQ studies, health, and spirituality to history, popular culture, time management, decluttering, lifestyle, mental wellness, aging, and sustainable living. We were recently named 20's #1 fastest growing independent publisher by *Publishers Weekly*. Our success is driven by our main goal, which is to publish high-quality books that will entertain readers as well as make a positive difference in their lives.

Our readers are our most important resource; we value your input, suggestions, and ideas. We'd love to hear from you—after all, we are publishing books for you!

Please stay in touch with us and follow us at:

Facebook: Mango Publishing
Twitter: @MangoPublishing
Instagram: @MangoPublishing
LinkedIn: Mango Publishing
Pinterest: Mango Publishing

Sign up for our newsletter at www.mangopublishinggroup.com and receive a free book!

Join us on Mango's journey to reinvent publishing, one book at a time.